New British Philosophy

New British Philosophy

Edited by Julian Baggini and Jeremy Stangroom

 LONDON AND NEW YORK

First published 2002
by Routledge
11 New Fetter Lane, London EC4P 4EE

Simultaneously published in the USA and Canada
by Routledge
29 West 35th Street, New York, NY 10001

Routledge is an imprint of the Taylor & Francis Group

© 2002 Edited by Julian Baggini and Jeremy Stangroom

Typeset in DIN and Minion by RefineCatch Limited, Bungay, Suffolk
Printed and bound in Great Britain by
TJ International Ltd, Padstow, Cornwall

British Library Cataloguing in Publication Data
A catalogue record for this book is available from the British Library

Library of Congress Cataloging in Publication Data
A catalog record for this book has been requested

ISBN 0–415–24345–9 (hbk)
ISBN 0–415–24346–7 (pbk)

Contents

The Philosophers

Keith Ansell Pearson

Professor of Philosophy at the University of Warwick

Tim Crane

Reader and Director of the Philosophy Programme at University College London, University of London

Roger Crisp

Tutor in Philosophy at the University of Oxford, and a Fellow of St Anne's College

Simon Critchley

Professor of Philosophy and Head of Department at the University of Essex, and Programme Director of the Collège Internationale de Philosophie in Paris

Miranda Fricker

Lecturer in Philosophy at Birkbeck College, University of London

Simon Glendinning

Lecturer in Philosophy at the University of Reading

Christina Howells

Professor of French at the University of Oxford, and a Fellow of Wadham College

Rae Langton

Professor of Moral Philosophy at the University of Edinburgh

Robin Le Poidevin

Professor of Metaphysics at the University of Leeds

Michael Martin

Lecturer in Philosophy at University College London, University of London

Ray Monk

Professor in Philosophy and Head of Department at the University of Southampton

Stephen Mulhall

Tutor in Philosophy at the University of Oxford, and a Fellow of New College

Aaron Ridley

Director of Postgraduate Studies in Philosophy at the University of Southampton, and Associate Director of the Centre for Post-Analytic Philosophy

Nigel Warburton

Senior Lecturer in Philosophy at The Open University

Timothy Williamson

Wykeham Professor of Logic at the University of Oxford, and a Fellow of New College

Jonathan Wolff

Professor of Philosophy and Head of Department at University College London, University of London

Preface

We would like to offer our thanks to the following people for their help in making this book possible. First, to the interviewees themselves, who did much more than just sit down and chat for a bit. Second, to the many philosophers who provided the recommendations for interviewees. Third, to the ever enthusiastic Routledge team: Tony Bruce, Muna Khogali and Aine Duffy. Fourth, the anonymous referees whose comments were valued even when ultimately ignored. Finally, to the friends, family, readers and supporters of *The Philosophers' Magazine*, whose general support has enabled us to work on this project.

Julian Baggini and Jeremy Stangroom

London, August 2001

Introduction

Contemporary Britain is fascinated by the nation's cultural barometer. The rise and fall of Britpop is charted in the broadsheet press as well as in the music glossies. People who rarely step inside an art gallery watch with fascination the progress of Tracey Emin, Gavin Turk, Damien Hurst and the rest of the Britart pack. The publication of *Granta*'s Best Young British Writers list also commands the attention of those who never have and never will read a single novel by any of the mentioned authors. And the fortunes of the British film industry, which ebb and flow with remarkable rapidity, are followed nearly as closely as those of the financial markets.

However, what is perhaps more interesting is which aspects of our culture escape our attention. When the *New Statesman* published its Best of Young Britain edition in July 2001, philosophers were conspicuous by their absence. Philosophers are among those who rarely move into the spotlight of popular scrutiny, and there are many explanations that can be given to account for this. Philosophy is, on the whole, slower moving than the arts. The trajectories of its star players follow more gently inclining, and declining, paths. Philosophers don't generally write with a broad public audience in mind – most of their work is directed at their professional peers. And philosophy is largely pursued within academia, a world not exactly designed to stir the hearts of the fashion-conscious mass media.

But there is a sense in which this lack of general awareness of the work of philosophers is regrettable. Despite the image of British philosophy during much of the twentieth century as a dry, stuffy, irrelevant discipline, the subject today is vibrant, diverse and thriving. Despite complaints about the restrictive and prescriptive nature of academic life, many young philosophers are managing to thrive within this hothouse and produce original and compelling work. What's more, key players are interested in presenting their work to a wider audience as well as to their fellow professionals. The result is that British philosophy today speaks to more people than at any time in its past.

There are several reasons for this. One is the increasing diversity of the subject. For many years, there were very few philosophy departments in Britain, and a few key centres dominated. This created, if not a hegemony, a kind of oligarchy, with the philosophers of Oxford, Cambridge and London very much setting the agenda for philosophy in the whole country. Now there are many more regional centres and greater scope for different styles of philosophy to flourish. Continental, postanalytic, feminist, interdisciplinary and applied philosophy all thrive where previously they were confined to the margins or not included at all.

There is also an increasing tendency to traverse the boundaries which previously separated particular schools of philosophy. More philosophers are drawing on contemporary work from both continental Europe and Britain, where before their interests were located in one or the other.

Philosophers have also become increasingly concerned to relate their work to what is going on in the 'real world'. This takes several forms. We have the continued rise of applied philosophy, with serious work being produced on bioethics, business ethics and public policy, for example. We have also seen more philosophers writing for the general public. That two Cambridge professors, Edward Craig and Simon Blackburn, should both be writing books for this readership is the most visible sign of a change of perception as to where the audience for philosophy may be.

The overall effect of these changes in British philosophy has been to make the subject more diverse, more exciting and more relevant to the concerns of more people. However, this change has gone largely unnoticed in the outside world. This is partly because of the traditional British disdain for the intellectual and partly because of the lack of nous of philosophers when it comes to communicating with a wider audience. It is also because there have been few opportunities for British philosophy to present itself to the outside world. There have been plenty of introductions to philosophy, but few opportunities to show off the work that is being done right here, right now.

One aim of this volume is to provide such a showcase. We believe that this is a particularly interesting time for British philosophy and that there are many people who will be stimulated, challenged and invigorated by reading what it has to offer. We do not expect the philosophers in this volume to become household names like Damon Albarn, Danny Boyle and Esther Freud, but we do think that what they have to say is of interest to many more people than just those taking philosophy degrees.

The State of British Philosophy

This book contains sixteen interviews with a wide range of British philosophers. Our selection is designed to show a representative range of the talents and interests among the generation of philosophers who are the heirs to the subject's aristocracy. We say more about how and why we chose the philosophers we did in the appendix. Here, we want to consider what the final list tells us about British philosophy today.

One striking feature is that, of the sixteen, only three are women. This does seem to be an accurate reflection of the state of British philosophy. For example, at the 2000 'Joint Session', the major UK conference for general philosophy, men outnumbered women by three to one. On the main programme, of the fifteen speakers only two were women, while just two out of the eight session chairs were women. There are signs of change, with many more young women holding academic positions and coming up through graduate studies. There has also been something of a breakthrough at Birkbeck College, London, where now nearly half its faculty are women philosophers. But at the present time, the number of women in this book reflects the sad truth that British philosophy has for a long time been dominated by males.

There are no black or minority ethnic philosophers in this book. Again, this just seems to be an accurate reflection of the demography of the subject. At the 'Joint Session' conference mentioned earlier, there were no black faces to be seen among the 150-odd delegates. For whatever reason, the subject has continued to attract predominantly white people.

There is, then, a sense in which the new diversity of British philosophy is limited. There may be fewer boundaries, more styles of philosophy being practised and more interdisciplinary work going on, but it is still mainly being done by white males (as this book was written and compiled by white males).

The geographical spread is also interesting. Half the interviewees come from the traditional bastions of the British philosophical establishment, the so-called 'golden triangle' of the universities of London, Oxford and Cambridge. But the other half come from a wide range of institutions: Warwick, Essex, Reading, Southampton, Leeds, Edinburgh and the Open University. This reflects the way in which regional centres of philosophy have increased in their importance. While the golden triangle still dominates, it is now possible to reach the top of the profession elsewhere.

The range of subjects covered in the interviews is also instructive. Several of the interviews cover what is known as 'continental' philosophy, by which is generally meant twentieth century French and German philosophy. Although the proportion of this kind of philosophy represented here is probably higher than the proportion of such philosophy researched and studied in British universities, it is nonetheless the case that more work is being done in continental philosophy than ever before. Further, as several interviewees make clear, the whole distinction between Anglo-American and continental philosophy has been problematised, with at least some now arguing that there is no fundamental distinction to be made between them.

This is a remarkable turnaround, when one considers that as recently as 1992, a proposal by Cambridge University to award an honorary degree to the French deconstructionist Jacques Derrida led to a petition being signed against it. Professor Barry Smith, in a letter to *The Times*, expressed a sentiment often voiced about continental philosophy in general, when he wrote: 'In the eyes of philosophers, and certainly among those working in leading departments of philosophy throughout the world, M. Derrida's work does not meet accepted standards of clarity and rigour.'

It would be untrue to suggest that there is not still hostility from many British philosophers to their continental counterparts, but there are many more seeking a rapprochement now than there were a decade ago.

The topics covered in this book reflect much of the work which is now going on in philosophy. Many familiar topics are included:

philosophy of mind, aesthetics, ethics, metaphysics, feminist theory and epistemology. Other interviews focus on styles of philosophy, such as the analytic, the continental and the post-analytic. We have also included a discussion about the popularisation of philosophy, because although this is not a topic in philosophy as such, it is a matter of increasing concern to philosophers who are seeking a wider audience for their work. Also represented is the emerging subject of philosophical biography.

Of course, this does not provide a comprehensive selection of all that is going on in the subject. There are no interviews on the philosophy of science, ancient philosophy or the history of philosophy, for instance. We make no apology for this. In order to keep the book down to a manageable size, some aspects of British philosophy were going to be left out which in an ideal world would not have been.

If the selection of people and topics in this book does not amount to a detailed anatomical drawing of the body of British philosophy today, it is also more than a mere snapshot of it. This volume should provide the reader with an accurate, if incomplete, impression of what philosophy in Britain is like today. Moreover, we hope that it will also give a sense of what philosophy will be like tomorrow, when the philosophers interviewed here, if they haven't already done so, take up their places at the very top of the profession.

How to Read this Book

The interviews have been arranged so that there is a natural progression in theme from one to the other. Each is preceded by a short introduction written by Baggini and Stangroom which provides some context for the discussion that follows. After each interview, a select bibliography includes five writings by the interviewee for those interested in reading more about their work. It is also possible to read any of the interviews independently of the others, or skip some altogether, although we do not, of course, advise that you do.

To facilitate flowing discussions, we did not ask interviewees to explain every difficult reference or allusion. Nor did we want to weigh down the text with explanatory footnotes. It should always be possible to follow the discussion without prior knowledge. But given the broad range of topics discussed, readers should expect the odd word, name, term of art or phrase to fly harmlessly over their heads, as they did on occasion with the interviewers.

1 Philosophical Biography

In conversation with Ray Monk

British philosophy has not traditionally taken much of an interest in the lives of its great figures. A recent graduate in the subject is likely to be familiar only with a few choice anecdotes, some apocryphal, some true.

So, for example, they may know that Nietzsche went mad, not because of his philosophy, but because of syphilis, and that his final breakdown saw him hugging an ass, sobbing; that Kant lived his whole life in Königsberg, where his walks were so regular that the women of the town set their clocks by them; that Wittgenstein once threatened Popper with a poker; that Descartes died prematurely when he contracted pneumonia while visiting Queen Christina of Sweden; that Socrates was condemned to death for corrupting the youth of Athens; and that Diogenes lived in a barrel and masturbated in public.

Biographical information about philosophers thus serves as no more than an amusing diversion. Give us anecdotes and tales of amusing foibles, but please, do not think biography could be important to philosophy itself.

This lack of interest in the lives of philosophers has its counterpart in the subject's history. The history of philosophy tends to be studied as if it were no more than an extended argument, a great conversation begun by Plato and Aristotle and continued up until the present day.

What does not get examined very often is the historical context within which the philosophers worked. The best scholars have always attended to these social and cultural factors, but more often than not they get placed to one side, especially in the teaching of the subject. Whereas it is commonplace in, say, the teaching of literature to begin a course on the nineteenth century novel with an examination of the society and culture of the time, a course on Descartes is more likely to begin with the text itself, or at most a reference to its philosophical antecedents.

What explains this relative lack of biographical and historical interest in British philosophy? Certain feminist critics argue that it is a product of a masculine conception of philosophy, where the self and the intellect are seen as independent, free-floating and autonomous. Men, who have denied the links between their intellectual pursuits and their bodies, gender and position in society, have dominated philosophy. Women, it is argued, are far more aware of the intimate link between how one thinks and rationalises, and one's nature as an embodied, socially and historically located individual. The ahistorical and non-biographical trend in philosophy merely reflects the male delusion that reason can be, and often is, separated from the individuals and societies within which it operates.

Whether or not one agrees wholeheartedly with this critique, at least part of it is undeniably true. That is to say, it is at least possible that what at first glance may appear to be detached, unbiased reasoning is largely a product of specific personal and social influences. Whether this undermines the philosophy or not is a further question. Whatever the answer to it, it does suggest that insight can be gained into the arguments of a philosopher by attending to those facts of their life and times.

Ray Monk is one of the few philosophers working in Britain today who has taken philosophical biography seriously. There are several biographies of philosophers available, but Monk's work stands out. For Monk, biography is not a diversion, but his core work. The bibliographies of many scholars contain a biography or two, but for Monk, biography has dominated his professional output for the best part of two decades, resulting in a life of Wittgenstein and two volumes on Bertrand Russell. These biographies are intended not only to tell interesting stories for their own sake, but to cast light on the philosophy of their subjects. Monk has related life and thought in a way which is extremely unusual in the British philosophical tradition. He is, therefore, something of a pioneer and it will be interesting to see whether one consequence of this is that we will see more philosophical biography in the twenty-first century than we did in the twentieth.

Philosophical biography is a specialism which didn't exist when you began your career. So how did you end up specialising in a specialism that didn't exist?

My postgraduate work was on Wittgenstein's philosophy of mathematics, and the way I got into biography was that I became convinced that almost all of the secondary literature on Wittgenstein's philosophy of mathematics misunderstood it. It misunderstood it in a particular kind of way. I felt that what was needed to correct the misunderstanding wasn't arguing piecemeal against one view after the other. It seemed to me that what was being missed was what you might call the spirit in which Wittgenstein wrote. It also seemed to me reading Wittgenstein, particularly the various draft prefaces he wrote to *Philosophical Remarks*, that he felt that acutely too. He felt that even the people who understood in a detailed way his views on this, that and the other, had missed his attitude to these questions. It seemed to me that one way of getting across the spirit in which Wittgenstein wrote would be to describe the life and the work alongside each other, so that one could read his work informed by some understanding of how he was writing and what attitudes were informing it.

That's interesting, because the philosophy of mathematics is one of the most abstract parts of philosophy and is therefore one which you would imagine you could treat with the least reference to a person's particular life.

In general that might be true, but in Wittgenstein's case it isn't. Some of his most passionate writing is on mathematics. He didn't just have an argument against logicism. He hated logicism. He described logicism as a cancerous growth. He talks about the disastrous invasion of mathematics by logic. Why did he feel so strongly about that? Because it's a symptom of what he perceived to be a more general cultural degeneration. When one understands that, one sees those remarks and the tone of them in the right context.

When you started out doing the philosophy of mathematics, presumably the way you were being taught and led did not push you towards the lives of the people behind it. So when you came to see those lives as important, did that seem like a major switch in the way you were thinking?

No. In my own case it went hand in hand with a more general disenchantment with academic philosophy. I left academic philosophy and did other things.

What was the root of the disenchantment?

The feeling that nothing serious was being said or entertained, but that a series of intellectual games were being pursued as a career.

Do you think that's still the case with most academic philosophy?

I think it's got a lot better. I'm talking now about the early 1980s, when I think British analytic philosophy was at its most arid. I went to a series of seminars in which the problem of adverbial predication was being discussed. This went on for about eight weeks, and the issue being discussed was this: if you say 'John walked up the hill slowly' it follows that John walked up the hill. If you say 'John walked up the hill quickly' it also follows that John walked up the hill. However, 'John walked up the hill slowly' implies not-'John walked up the hill quickly', and the problem was to devise a way of preserving those inferential relations. Well, what interest does this have? I found myself thinking that the pleasure one derives from those kinds of problems has no more depth to it than the pleasure one derives from a crossword puzzle.

You obviously admire Russell's early work in the philosophy of mathematics, and some people might ask what the point of that is – trying to explain how all of mathematics can be explained purely in terms of logic. That might also seem to be a nice intellectual game to play.

But one has to understand what he thought he was doing. He thought that he was laying bare the most general features of reality. We don't believe he was doing that, but if we did, it would be a tremendously important thing. The people pursuing adverbial predication were not animated by the passion that Russell was animated by, which is the feeling that they're discovering something about reality. That seemed to me missing. What was going on here was that an intellectual puzzle was being pursued because it was a diverting intellectual puzzle.

Does it really matter what's motivating people? You seem to be saying that the motivation is important to the value of the end

product. Some people might be motivated purely in the way that someone else is motivated by a crossword puzzle, but you don't know where these things will lead in philosophy. It's always worth going away and studying these things, because what might look like a bit of scholastic debate might actually end up leading to something which crucially changes our understanding.

Yes, but you're asking why I was disenchanted with analytic philosophy. It was because of the motivation, not the end result. I didn't feel part of a community that was interested in understanding things worth understanding.

Thinking a little more about how learning about someone's life might help you understand their philosophy, it might seem surprising that it is even possible. For example, you wouldn't think you would learn something important about quantum theory by looking at the lives of scientists who formulated it. So you wouldn't see there being any scientific interest in the lives of scientists. Where is the philosophical interest in the lives of philosophers?

It varies from philosopher to philosopher, I think. It's almost certainly not true that light can be shed on every philosopher's work by consideration of their life. I've yet to read anything about Kant's life that was enormously revealing about his work, whereas I think with Wittgenstein and Russell, much can be learned in different ways by looking at their work in the context of their lives.

With Wittgenstein, you talked about the spirit of his work. What is that spirit of his life and work?

It's summed up in the remark 'logic and ethics are fundamentally the same'. There are two very striking facts about Wittgenstein. On the ethics side, he pared his life down to the minimum, so as to make as central as possible his search for decency, the drive to be a decent person. That is one of the most conspicuous and striking things about Wittgenstein. Whether you think he was a decent person or not, you can see that a lot of things he did were motivated by this drive. On the logic side, he had a relentless drive for clarity. It seems to me that in Wittgenstein's case, one can see that these are two sides of the same coin, that he thought one couldn't achieve clarity unless one achieved decency. He remarked to Russell that thinking about logic and thinking about his sins were simultaneous. In a remark in a letter to Russell, he asks, 'How can I be a logician before I'm a decent human being?' He thought what got in the way of thinking clearly was as often as not vanity, a refusal to come clean with oneself.

To acknowledge that helps understand where the philosophy is coming from and what's motivating it. It's presumably a fallacy to move from that to saying that you can actually judge the philosophical end result by looking at the biography. Would you want to maintain the traditional view that the validity or otherwise of the philosophical position can be judged independently of any facts about the life of the philosopher?

Well, yes. But often what that shows is how little is gained by judging the validity of a philosophical position. But surely it's true that whether the proofs of the *Principia* are valid or not cannot in any way depend on any facts about Russell's life.

You've indicated that there are limitations on judging validity. Some might think that's all you have to do. If we talk about arguments being sound rather than valid, you might think all you have to do is look at the arguments and if they work, they work, and if they don't, they don't – end of philosophy.

No, I don't think so. Philosophy would be a very arid business if that were the case. The great philosophers are those with insight, insight into something important. Of course, when one's teaching students, one says 'Don't just give me your conclusion, give me arguments'. But who reads Nietzsche, who reads Wittgenstein, who reads Kierkegaard, laying it out as if it were a piece of propositional calculus, and says this argument goes through or it doesn't? It would be impossibly boring and would miss the point.

A problem with training students in the way that we do is that we encourage them to be concerned with whether an argument is valid or not, and we don't encourage them very much to consider the question of whether the argument is interesting or not. You can see the results of that in academic journals. When I'm sent articles to provide a reader's report on for journals, more often than not the editor will want to know: Does this article show that the person is up to date with the reading? Is this argument a novel contribution to the literature? Is this argument sound? They don't want to know if it's very boring.

Let's turn to your first biography of Wittgenstein. He's a great subject in lots of ways because he led a very singular life, yet he also conforms to the stereotype of the tortured genius. There's a remark he makes on his death bed which is perhaps surprising given what's come before. He says, 'Tell them I've had a wonderful life'. How does that fit in with the fact that he seemed to have had a remarkably difficult, troubled life? Did it surprise you when you first heard of it?

It didn't surprise me particularly. One would be loath to regard that as Wittgenstein's definitive comment, a summation of his life. It was a remark made at a particular moment, for a particular audience; tell *them* I've had a wonderful life. It seemed to me the kind of thing that

Wittgenstein would want said to his closest friends. But I also think he thought he had indeed, in some ways, had a wonderful life. And indeed it was a wonderful life.

In what respects? Not in the sense that it was more enjoyable than most, for example.

No, but Wittgenstein achieved a kind of purity of purpose that very few of us achieve. That's one of the things that makes him so fascinating. A lot of the things that occupy my time – about my kids, about my mortgage, about day to day life – Wittgenstein successfully eliminated from his life, and that gives his life a kind of archetypal purity and concentration. There's something wonderful about that. It would have surprised me if he had said, 'Tell them I've had a happy life'.

Something strikes me as similar about Wittgenstein and Russell's philosophical lives and careers. Both in their earlier philosophies were trying to set out something that was pretty systematic and logically complete, in different spheres. They then came to see these attempts as failures, though how they moved on from that differed. Did it colour your view of the subject when you looked at two of the greatest philosophical minds of the last century and saw that they both, for different reasons, came to the conclusion that it was not possible to give a fully consistent, systemised account of key major areas in philosophy?

I don't think so. Perhaps it confirmed my view of philosophy. It does make them particularly interesting figures, because one then wants to understand what hopes were being thwarted. The hope that was being thwarted in Wittgenstein's case was the hope of achieving complete crystalline clarity, and the hope that was being thwarted in Russell's case was the hope of achieving complete certainty. I think there's

something revealing in that contrast about why we do philosophy. Do
we do philosophy because we want absolutely certain foundations for
everything we believe, as Russell did; or do we do philosophy because
we feel it muddled, a bit confused, and we want this confusion
dispelled?

**Both of these people, whose abilities outstrip those of most of us,
concluded that we couldn't have either of those things. Have the
consequences of those failures been taken to heart by philosophers
practising today?**

I'm not sure I see philosophy like that, as it were, learning from other
people's mistakes. Perhaps you could. But what would taking that on
board mean? It might mean going through that process yourself. It
doesn't go without saying that you could take up where Wittgenstein
left off. To understand Wittgenstein or Russell's work, you might have
to be tempted by the aspirations that motivated them and then perhaps
see that this complete certainty, this complete clarity, is a chimera.

**Did you share either of those motivations when you first got
into philosophy?**

More Wittgenstein's than Russell's. More to do with wanting clarity
than certainty.

**How has that been shaped by your studies, particularly of Wittgen-
stein? How have you come out the other end of that?**

I suppose by thinking that clarification is a process, not a state. This is
wherein lies the virtue of philosophy, despite all the boring stuff which
is done in its name. Why do we do philosophy? Because there is a
process of clarification and this is a good thing. A really good tutorial
session, a really good seminar, is when the students come with some-

thing which is bothering them and they leave the room slightly clearer about what that is than before. But they haven't achieved any final state. Hopefully, what they've done is think through something which is now a bit clearer.

Wittgenstein's reaction to his earlier failure was to come back with a different type of philosophy. The work of the later Wittgenstein really does divide people. There are people who worship the man and others who despise him. But both of them might agree that Wittgenstein in a sense turned his back on philosophy as we know it. How radical do you think his break with the philosophical tradition he had both been educated in and contributed to was?

Very radical indeed, to the point where, to be a Wittgensteinian philosopher, in the sense of the late Wittgenstein is more or less incompatible with pursuing philosophy as a career.

Would you consider yourself to be a Wittgensteinian in that sense?

I think one of the important lessons to be learned from the later Wittgenstein is that philosophy is not a science and not a bit like a science. Philosophy is a process and as such the apparatus that goes with a modern academic discipline sits very uneasily on philosophy. A Ph.D. degree, for example, has some kind of sense in science. If you imagine science as putting little building blocks in place, you can see a Ph.D. degree as making a contribution to that structure. In philosophy, we have the form but not the content. People do Ph.D. degrees, and it's supposed to be that they make a contribution to the literature, they put another little brick in place in the structure, but actually this makes no sense at all in philosophy. The same is true with what's described as 'the literature' – contributing papers to academic journals. All that implicitly assumes that there is a structure being built, and there just isn't in philosophy, if one takes a Wittgensteinian view of it.

The reason I'm interested in this is that you haven't rejected academic philosophy entirely, in that you have an academic position, but at the same time you have a lot of sympathy for Wittgenstein. I wonder whether there's a certain balancing act going on here and how comfortable you are with it.

Well, the answer is that there is a balancing act going on and that there are many aspects of academic life that I'm uncomfortable with. Research assessment, the way articles are published, the way degrees are given – actually most of it!

So what keeps you in it?

Because it's where philosophy goes on. It needn't be. There's no reason why what I value in philosophy can't go on outside academic life. But as it happens, if you want to pursue philosophy and teach philosophy, then you end up in an academic life.

Turning to Russell, he was clearly a very able philosopher. But outside of the particular area of the philosophy of mathematics, he didn't seem to do very well at all. His political reasoning seemed to be extremely inept. A lot of people try to sell philosophy these days by saying that it gives you transferable thinking skills. But the evidence from Russell and Wittgenstein seems to be that there aren't many transferable skills there. They seemed to be very good at thinking about certain things but not necessarily any good at all at thinking about others. Do you think that looking at the lives of these people does undermine the idea that philosophy teaches you a transferable skill?

Not entirely, no. But it's certainly true that a lot of Russell's work outside philosophy is just rubbish, ill-considered and sloppily written. People talk about what a wonderful writer Russell was, but of the literally thousands of articles he published, there are quite a lot which are badly written, badly thought out, where he gives vent to his prejudices, he doesn't consider relevant aspects of the question he is dealing with and so on. His writings on politics, marriage and ethics – there's an awful lot there which is just bad.

Does this undermine the idea that if you're good at philosophy you'll be good at thinking through other things? Not entirely. What it does show is that you can't adopt the kind of arrogance that Russell adopted and say, I've thought about the most difficult problem that there is, and so working out who should be the next president of the United States will be a piece of cake. It doesn't work like that. But neither does it mean that thinking clearly is a waste of time or that studying philosophy doesn't help you think clearly. Studying philosophy does help you think clearly, but then whether you do think clearly or not is a matter of will.

The question of how he published such poor work troubles you throughout the book. But you don't seem to have satisfied yourself with an answer.

No. There's not going to be a simple answer, but one thing is this: Could he have written better about politics, about marriage, about happiness? Yes, he could. So the question is not why he was so limited in those areas, but why he set himself such low standards.

But do you really think he could have written much better about marriage? It did seem that when it came to conducting his personal life, he basically lacked a certain set of people skills. It wasn't

anything to do with his lack of reasoning abilities. He just didn't seem to understand personal relationships and the manner in which matters of the heart affect people, in the kind of way that is necessary to be able to talk about these things. He didn't have the emotional insight into people which would enable him to apply his intellectual abilities in a constructive way.

I think that's largely true. The other thing is that he was to a certain extent hampered by his philosophical abilities, or at least by his philosophy, which drew too rigid a distinction between the contrast you made – affairs of the heart, on one hand, and reasoning, on the other. Russell felt, I think, that anything that couldn't be satisfied by a valid deductive argument was just settled by the whim of feeling. That is to say, he is too ready to assume that feelings are just irrational and there's no doing anything about it. So if he wakes up one morning and discovers that he's not in love with Alys, that's it. All he can do is live with that and then get Alys to live with that. The idea that one could reason this through, ask what's happening with his marriage to Alys, why this sudden break, all those sort of things don't occur to him because he assumes that affairs of the heart are essentially and irretrievably irrational.

You talked earlier about Russell's arrogance, that having thought about the hardest questions imaginable, he had carte blanche to talk about anything else. Do you think that's an arrogance which is not untypical of philosophers?

I'm not sure. You might say that one of the reasons why philosophy is so unexciting at the moment is that British philosophers have become too humble in that respect. They work away on their little problems and they're reluctant to say anything about other things. Even the ones that do, do so in their spare time. They write their philosophy books and then they publish journalism, and they don't attach much importance to the latter. Or if they do, it exhibits some of the arrogance you speak of – here am I a logician and I'm going to tell you what to think about the current debate about education, and so on. But in general, I think philosophy has become too isolated from life outside the academy.

I want to finish by turning to the future a bit. You're still pretty much a one-man ghetto, in that though others with philosophical backgrounds have written biographies of philosophers, what you've done with the three books is pretty much unique. Do you see any sign that as a discipline within the subject, philosophical biography might be taken more seriously?

There are signs of that, yes. One sign of that is the number of conferences I get invited to devoted to the subject of biography and philosophers. They tend to be interdisciplinary. They tend to involve people from philosophy and English departments, with some people from history, politics and whatever. There also tend to be one-man ghettos in disciplines such as politics who write biographies of political figures. I've been to five or six conferences – and thinking about philosophy in relation to biography, particularly in the States, is becoming a tiny little subgenre. I'm not entirely comfortable with that, because for me, one of the virtues of biography is that it's a non-theoretical enterprise. If you then start contributing to the theory of biography you've pulled the rug from under yourself.

That's interesting, because some people would say there is a philosophical question about how one can tell the truth of a life.

I don't mean at all that there aren't interesting philosophical issues to do with biography. Of course there are, they're interesting and they interest me and I have written on them and so on. I just mean that the idea of a theory of biography is appalling.

Are you working on anyone else now?

I'm going to write a book about philosophy and biography and a book about Wittgenstein's philosophy of mathematics. But the next biography I'm going to write is of a scientist, Robert Oppenheimer. It seems to me that one could do a philosophical biography of Oppenheimer. What makes a philosophical biography? Sartre wrote philosophical biographies of literary figures, Baudelaire and Flaubert. What makes something a philosophical biography needn't be that it's the biography of a philosopher, just somebody where there is some dynamic, an interaction to reveal and describe, between somebody's preoccupation with ideas and their life. I think that's the case with Oppenheimer. What makes a biography philosophical is that it shows the interplay between thought and life.

Select Bibliography

'Philosophical biography: the very idea', in *Wittgenstein: Biography and Philosophy*, edited by J. Klagge, Cambridge University Press, 2001

Bertrand Russell Volume 1: The Spirit of Solitude, Jonathan Cape, 1996

Bertrand Russell Volume 2: The Ghost of Madness, Jonathan Cape, 2000

'Was Russell an analytical philosopher?', *Ratio*, 9: 3, 1996

Ludwig Wittgenstein: The Duty of Genius, Jonathan Cape, 1990

2 Ethics in the Modern World

In conversation with Roger Crisp

'How are we to live?' has been a central question in philosophy since the birth of the subject. Ethics is the branch of the discipline that seeks to answer it. There is a standard way of dividing up the most important general approaches in ethics, which Roger Crisp refers to as the 'Philosophy 101' account, in reference to the first-year undergraduate courses that introduce students to the distinctions. This standard view divides ethical theories into three broad types: consequentialist, Kantian and virtue ethics.

The consequentialist approach links the rightness or wrongness of actions with the goodness or badness of their consequences. So, for example, an action which has only good consequences must be preferred to an action which has only bad consequences. In any given circumstance, to answer the question 'what is the morally right act?', one need only see which act would have the best consequences.

Of course, to put this into practice, one needs a clear idea of what good and bad consequences are. The most popular ethical theory to flesh out this idea is utilitarianism, developed by, for example, Jeremy Bentham and John Stuart Mill. Utilitarians claim that right actions are those which result in the 'greatest happiness of the greatest number', while wrong actions fail to do this. Some later utilitarians rejected this hedonistic conception of the good and argued that we should be increasing people's capacities to live according to their preferences, whether this makes them happier or not. Many other versions of utilitarianism have also been developed.

In contrast, the Kantian (or 'deontological') view places the idea of duty at the heart of ethics. To act morally is to do what duty demands, irrespective of what the consequences may be. Some acts, such as torture, for example, are just morally wrong, even if on a particular occasion they might lead to the best consequences. Torture cannot be morally justified, even if by torturing someone we find out information that can save thousands of people. The ends do not justify the means.

On Kant's view, we do not need to consider the consequences of an act to see if it is the morally right one. We just need to follow a principle he calls the categorical imperative, namely, 'Act only on that maxim which you can at the same time will to become a universal law'. A Kantian might argue that, since one could not will that it become universally acceptable for people to torture to extract useful information, one cannot morally justify torturing someone for the greater good.

The third broad tradition is that of virtue ethics, which many trace back to the work of Aristotle. The focus here is neither acts nor consequences, but character. The virtuous person must cultivate a character which enables human flourishing.

One reason for putting character at the centre of ethics is that people act according to habit. If we want to live well, we are better equipped to do so if we have the kind of character that, by habit, disposes us towards certain virtuous courses of actions, ones which enable human flourishing. So, for example, the virtuous person will tend not to lie, not because they calculate that the consequences of lying will be bad, nor because they recognise they are compelled to do so by the moral law, but because they have developed their character in such a way as to make lying anathema.

However, as with so much in philosophy, real ethics is much more complicated than this Philosophy 101 division of the subject suggests. The work of Roger Crisp explores these complications and it is Crisp's contention that the tripartite division of ethics, though useful in introductory courses, does not reflect the true nature of the subject itself.

Crisp is also interested in going beyond theory and into practice. After the logical positivists claimed in the 1920s and 1930s that most ethics was literally meaningless, Anglo-Saxon philosophy became far removed from real-life moral dilemmas. This trend has been reversed in recent years and many philosophers have been working on issues in applied ethics. Crisp's interests weld together a serious concern with the complexity of ethical theory with a practical concern for its application outside academia.

Your first brush with philosophy was not a happy one. How did you nonetheless end up coming to philosophy?

I studied classics at Oxford, which involves ancient literature, ancient history, and philosophy, modern as well as ancient. I remember trying to give up philosophy the first time I did it. I was told to read Locke's *Essay on Human Understanding*, which I did. The problem was that I read an abridged version with no introduction. I hadn't spoken to my tutor about it to help me see what Locke was trying to do, and I just couldn't make sense of it. Was it science? Well, there didn't seem to be any experiments. It wasn't literature, because he wasn't just making it up. So I couldn't understand the questions he was trying to answer. I still find that with students the initial hurdle in philosophy is to understand what the question is.

I tried to find my tutor so I could give up philosophy and do literature instead. I couldn't find her so I continued with it. Then we had a term on ethics in which I read Mill's *On Liberty*. That converted me to philosophy, because he was writing about questions I had tried to think about myself, questions like: What's wrong with censorship? Why is it important that people should be allowed to wear silly clothes? That mattered to me, having been to a school where I wasn't allowed to wear silly clothes!

Moral philosophy and ethics have remained a core interest for you. Students are usually taught that there are three broad traditions in ethical thought: virtue ethics, Kantian or deontological ethics and utilitarian ethics. How accurate do you think these distinctions are?
I think that it's not as easy to draw these distinctions between utilitarianism, Kantianism and virtue ethics as people think. Quite often when someone comes up with a characterisation, you'll find that it doesn't carve the theories at the right points, and actually the characterisation that's being given could apply as easily to any theory.

For example, a virtue theorist might say character should be primary in ethics. But there's nothing to stop a utilitarian also saying character should be primary in ethics, and that the only virtue that matters is benevolence. That's a standard way of arguing for utilitarianism, usually through the notion of an ideal spectator.

So rather than being distinct categories of very different ways of doing moral philosophy, it's more to do with what the primary focus is?
Well, again, that doesn't really distinguish the theories. I think the distinctions are useful, but they're a bit like the distinctions you get told about when you do GCSE, and then do the A-level and find it's not

quite like that. I think for Philosophy 101 it's very useful to be told there are these three traditions, utilitarianism, Kantianism and virtue ethics. What worries me is when you get people writing in journals as if those distinctions are clear cut and there's a consensus on what they amount to. And what is even more worrying is when people start slotting particular thinkers under one heading or another. So Hume, people say, is or is not a utilitarian.

I want to talk a little about utilitarianism because you've done some quite specific work on that. Broadly, utilitarianism is a consequentialist theory. How would you characterise consequentialism or how do you see the traditional characterisation as being at fault?

I can tell you what I think is wrong with the notion of consequentialism as an idea. It assumes that there is agreement about when an act ends and when its consequences begin. Of course, there can't be agreement on that, because it all depends on the description of the act that you're using. So, for example, it's very common for people to say that utilitarians don't care about the nature of the action you're performing, whether, say, it's killing or not. All they care about are the consequences and whether they're the best from a utilitarian point of view or not. But in a sense utilitarians might not care about consequences at all. There is just one action that they think you should perform: you should maximise utility. The consequences may be that a lot of people die or lots of people suffer, but they don't care about that. That way of carving up so-called consequentialist and non-consequentialist positions sounds good but it doesn't work.

What's wrong with the characterisation of a utilitarian as someone who believes one should do whatever act has the consequence of increasing utility?

You can do it like that; that's fine. But I could equally characterise a deontologist, who believes killing is always wrong, as someone who thinks you should never do any act which has the consequence of killing somebody. So again it's a logical failure – it doesn't capture the differences between the two views.

The differences between the two views might seem to be captured first of all in what they tell you to do. But that often isn't enough because utilitarians might say that on utilitarian grounds you should live a virtuous life, which makes them sound like virtue theorists. You've got to get behind what they say to find out why they say it. But you shouldn't assume that, if you do, you're going the find a single story. For example, I think there's a huge difference between ancient and modern virtue ethics. If you asked Aristotle why I should be virtuous he'd say, 'For your own happiness – your happiness consists in being virtuous and nothing else'. No modern thinker says that. Most of them say you should be virtuous because you should. So in that sense they're like the people who call themselves deontologists.

Isn't one problem with saying 'utilitarianism is a consequentialist ethic' that it sets up a straw person, because critics focus narrowly on consequences, whereas actually a utilitarian has to take into account the way in which character, sense of duty and so on impact on utility?

That seems to me dead right and something like that is exactly the criticism Mill made of Bentham in the essay 'On Bentham' when he said 'Bentham was a boy to the last' – because he didn't reflect enough upon the sophistication and the subtlety of human imagination and the importance of character to ethics. So it's not as if virtue ethics identified the importance of character first.

In your book on Mill you say that the first step to utilitarianism is to accept that the morally right action is the one that increases welfare. You use the word 'welfare' rather than 'utility'. Why do you use 'welfare' and why do you prefer it over 'utility'?

I take welfare to be, in a sense, a formal notion, equivalent to what Aristotle called 'eudaimonia', which is often translated as 'happiness' or 'the good'. In that sense, it's just a placeholder. It's a trivial point to say that what we're all after or what we should be after is welfare. The interesting question is what it consists in. And then you get the different theories. The way people carve it up now standardly is that welfare consists in pleasure, or desire satisfaction of some kind, or some set of goods in addition to pleasure. That's a useful Philosophy 101 way of carving things up. There are ways of getting behind it and making it more subtle, but it does the trick to start with.

Classical utilitarianism says that welfare is about maximising happiness and minimising suffering. This hedonist theory is seen by many as being too narrow in its conception. Do you agree with those critics?

Well, I've changed my view since writing the book on Mill. I've started to reflect on the basis of the beliefs I had which led me to reject hedonism, and they seem to me to be rather similar in standing to the beliefs which constitute common-sense morality. But I don't myself have much time for common-sense morality. If we reject common-sense views of morality and common-sense views of welfare, then what we're left with, I think, is hedonism as almost certainly partly right.

I think it must be almost undeniable that pleasure is part of what makes life good. And then the question is, 'Is there anything else?' Is, say, accomplishing something in your life important? Typically, this thought is followed by arguments debunking the hedonist view, and that worries me, as there are debunking arguments against common-sense morality. Very simple, obviously highly fictional, but not implausible accounts can be given to explain common-sense morality. People like Matt Ridley have brought this out recently. You can see why a group with something like our common-sense morality is going to do better in terms of survival. It seems the same is going to be true of a group in which individuals within that group are praised for working hard or accomplishing something. So that raises the question of whether there is any basis to those beliefs, or whether the sensible guys aren't just the ones who sit back in the cave and enjoy themselves while the others go out and do the work.

This is a really interesting issue because it raises the question of how you decide between competing moral theories. What you're saying is that the evidence against the hedonistic view is based on common-sense intuitions about what the good life consists in, and because you've got reason to doubt common sense, then you've got reason to at least doubt the validity of those kinds of arguments. When you're trying to assess two or more competing moral theories, what is the ultimate arbiter if it's not something like common sense? You could put in consistency perhaps, but assuming many different moral views are all consistent – you can't just debunk them on the basis that they're self-defeating – how do you then decide between them?

That's a very good question. I'd like to stipulate that by common sense I mean something unreflective. So common-sense beliefs are just beliefs we've been brought up to have and we haven't reflected on. Now they may be correct, of course. Just because we haven't reflected on them doesn't mean they're not right. Then you've got to start reflecting on these beliefs. Some people like Rawls say that all you've got to do is get these unreflective beliefs into some kind of equilibrium with reflective principles. That does seem to me to be a bit of a mistake. I think what one really ought to do is, first of all, to try to understand what beliefs one has and try to make them as precise as possible. You then try to understand where they come from, and that's where the history of morality as opposed to the history of moral philosophy is important, and that's something we haven't made nearly enough progress towards. So these arguments I've called debunking arguments may not turn out to be debunking arguments. If we found out people could only do maths now because, in caves, people had to be able to divide up food, you wouldn't say, 'Oh, then maths must be a mistake'. It could be that the debunking arguments fail and common sense remains as it is.

The final stage would be a stage of reflection. Here, in a real sense you're trying to distance yourself from a commitment to any of these beliefs, and you're just trying to work out which is most plausible. This is something like the method Henry Sidgwick advocated in his book, *The Methods of Ethics*. It's a kind of intuitionism and I think it's interesting that intuitionism is coming back into popularity, certainly in Britain and the US, in a kind of sanitised form because it's no longer tied to theism or any kind of dogmatism. It's just tied to the idea that progress in ethics is made through reflection.

Moving to more general issues, most people believe that post-war moral philosophy in Britain had an aversion to dealing with real moral issues, instead concentrating on things like whether one had a duty to post a letter or not. Do you think that's a fair characterisation of the past of moral philosophy, and if so how did moral philosophy become so divorced from any concern with real life?
I think it's something of an exaggeration to say that moral philosophers

had nothing to say about matters of general concern. People like Ayer and Hare had things to say about the issues of their day. But there was certainly less interest than there is now. Why was that? Well, I suspect that what was really responsible was logical positivism and the doubt that threw on the whole notion of ethics, through the work of people like Ayer. If you seriously believe emotivism – that moral judgements are just expressions of emotion and nothing else – you are going to find it less serious as an enterprise. You're going to start thinking of your moral judgements as being tastes, and why should you try to convert other people to your tastes? Obviously, more subtle emotivists tried to explain why, but somehow their views didn't really hold water.

The other factor would be the ordinary language school of philosophy, people like Austin, who thought that if you're going to do ethics, the first thing to do is to start understanding the way that moral words are used in ordinary language. That's a way of doing philosophy, but if you're doing that you haven't got time to think about using the words themselves in discussion of particular concrete issues.

Then we had the rise of applied philosophy in America, post-Vietnam, when people saw moral philosophy as containing a huge vacuum where thought didn't engage with real issues. In the history of ethics, from the earliest times, people did it because, as Aristotle said, there's no point in doing ethics unless you want to become a better person.

Do you really think that the growth of applied ethics in this country has its roots in the American experience of Vietnam?
Yes I do. What was particularly interesting about the rise of applied ethics in America was the high quality of philosophy that was done in that area of writing from the start. You only have to look at the first few issues of *Philosophy and Public Affairs* to see that. That was very

important because now there's a lot of really bad work being done in applied philosophy, and if that had been done in the beginning it wouldn't have been taken as seriously as it is now.

Without people agreeing on their abstract ethical principles, it would seem that there isn't enough basic agreement about assumptions to make progress on applied issues. But equally, if agreement on those abstract theories is required in order to discuss the applied debate, you won't get agreement because people in fact embrace different approaches. So how do you get progress in applied ethics?

Personally, I think you can make real progress in ethics only at the level of theory. So if we just say that we're going to forget about theory and trade common-sense intuitions about problems, we're not going to get anywhere. The point is that by thinking about particular cases we will advance our theories and that's how we'll make progress.

Also, many of the debates within these particular areas are not issuing out of head-to-head clashes between the popular moral theories that are around. Take, for example, the debate which dominates environmental ethics: whether the environment has value in itself. That isn't really a debate between Kantianism, virtue ethics or utilitarianism. It's a debate about the nature of value. But there are theories about that, and the way to resolve the debate is to come up with a theory of value.

There was an interesting example in the United States where six philosophers produced an amicus brief for the Supreme Court on euthanasia. Looking at them as philosophers, there's quite a lot of disagreement among them on moral theory. Yet they could agree on quite a lengthy document about a particular topic. Was that just a bit of good luck or does it tell us something more?

I think it tells us that there's a lot more agreement between people than they like to think. People rather enjoy the cut and thrust of philosophical debate. But often, when you get down to brass tacks, there's a lot more common ground than people realise, partly because they don't understand the ground they themselves are standing on. That's one reason why one might want to encourage practical ethics. You might ask what the point is of doing applied ethics, if everyone disagrees about ethical theory. Well, actually, though they might be disagreeing a little bit about ethical theory, there's less disagreement than they think. And also they tend to converge on various conclusions. In environmental ethics, for example, most people think that we are wrecking the environment in ways which we shouldn't be and they're coming out with arguments why we should stop. Philosophy aside, that's surely something we want to encourage.

How much are philosophers who engage in applied ethics required to get a good knowledge of the world with which they're dealing? For example, in business ethics, if the phrase 'cash flow' means nothing to me except for the fact that at the end of the month I haven't got much money, and that after pay day, I'm all right for a bit, can I do business ethics?

There are two extreme views here, both of which I think are wrong. One is that philosophy is an abstract enterprise, so you don't need to know anything about these areas before you say something about them. The other view is that you can't say anything philosophically about business ethics unless you're pretty clued up about the nature of business. Both of these seem to me false. It depends very much on the nature of the question you're trying to answer. If you're trying to answer a very abstract question, such as what the nature of business in modern society should be, or even a metaphysical question, such as whether the notion of a corporation is analogous in various ways to that of a person, you don't need to know how corporations work. But if you're trying to answer questions about how corporations actually operate, then you do need to know the facts. It gives philosophy a bad name if people don't bother to find out those facts.

Thinking of the future, how are you, on a personal level, going to try to continue your balance of interests between the applied and the more theoretical issues in ethics?

One thing that worries me about modern philosophy is the specialisation and professionalisation that exist in the subject, which contrast so strongly with what was going on at the beginning of the twentieth century. When you build into that the pressure to publish that now exists both here and in the United States, I'm worried that people are losing touch with the past. At the beginning of the twentieth century, it would have been quite possible for a serious moral philosopher to read almost everything that was thought to be important as it came out, and they could also be familiar with the great writers of the past. That's becoming more and more difficult. I think there's a natural bias that human beings seem to have towards contemporary thought, which itself is philosophically questionable. More and more attention is paid to the latest article in *Ethics*, and less and less attention is paid to, for example, the British Moralists, people like Shaftesbury and Hutcheson and so on. So one thing I'd really like to do is read those people properly, think about them, see what I can learn from them, and see if there are contributions I could make on the basis of that to contemporary moral philosophy.

The second thing I'm interested in is the idea of the self. It's really just developing the line of thought that Bernard Williams began in his critique of utilitarianism and Kantianism. The ancient ideal of showing that self-interest and morality are one and the same, I think, is pretty well a non-starter. I'm not absolutely sure about that and I want to think about it more. I suspect that it is a dream we'll have to give up. Then the question arises, as it did originally for the Greeks, how we handle these two facts: I have a life to live, and so does everyone else. It's just too easy to say, as the utilitarians do, 'Just ignore your own life, it doesn't matter, you've got no special reason to give it priority'. It's too easy to say, 'Forget about everybody else', or take the Kantian line that morality is just overriding. So what I want to do is start thinking about that question, perhaps in the light of thinking about the British Moralists, but also relating it to the thoughts of people like Bernard Williams and many other people who have recognised this problem.

In science, people say that knowledge converges and you gain consensus. We've had over two thousand years of ethical thought in our tradition and there doesn't seem to be much convergence going on. How would you answer the sceptic who says that we've run our course in understanding ethics? We know what the options are now; there's not going to be more convergence. As a research project, there's nothing left for the future of ethics.

That's the pessimistic view that one finds at the end of the earlier editions of Sidgwick's *Methods of Ethics*, that practical reason is a kind of chaos, and we can no longer make any progress because there are just these irresolvable disagreements. But I rather agree with the optimistic tone that Derek Parfit takes at the end of *Reasons and Persons*, that though it is true that ethics has been done for thousands of years, the kind of secular ethics that we do has really only been done for a few hundred years. There has been some convergence on some matters, in life as a whole and not just in philosophy. It just seems to me to be intellectually lazy to give up and say, 'That's the end of the road; we might as well give up'. What we should do is keep trying as hard as we can to come up with consensus on abstract principles of ethics. If we had already been trying for thousands of years, then I'd be more pessimistic. Then I'd perhaps think that we'd have to go for some kind of pluralism and that there might be something to be said for several of these positions and we just have to judge in particular cases which should apply. Or you might even start thinking in terms of some genuine indeterminacy. But, as things are, I think that we've got a good chance of coming up with some set of principles.

Select Bibliography

'Sidgwick and the boundaries of intuitionism', in *Essays on Intuitionism*, edited by P. Stratton-Lake, Oxford University Press, 2002

'Particularizing particularism', in *Moral Particularism*, edited by B. Hooker and M. Little, Oxford University Press, 2000

Virtue Ethics (edited with M. Slote), Clarendon Press, 1997

Mill on Utilitarianism, Routledge, 1997

'A good death: Who best to bring it?' *Bioethics*, 1: 1, 1987

3 The Role of Political Philosophy

In conversation with Jonathan Wolff

Political philosophy occupies a curious position in the intellectual landscape. On the one hand, as a branch of philosophy, it deals with general, theoretical issues, eschewing the practical questions of, for example, how to administer a social security system. On the other, as a branch of politics, it is part of a sphere of human activity which is almost by definition engaged in the real world. There is thus a kind of tension within the subject between the essential engagement of politics and the frequent disengagement of the philosopher.

To what extent is political philosophy separate from the rough and tumble of politics? The subject matter of political philosophy in the Anglophone world has traditionally been the nature of certain general concepts and principles, such as liberty, rights, equality and the legitimacy of the state. These issues have a perennial nature. Pick up Plato's *Republic* or Aristotle's *Politics* and you will find the roots of the current debates about them there.

If we take liberty as an example, the philosopher's interest is in liberty's most general nature. She would ask questions such as: 'What does it mean to say that a person should be allowed liberty? Is liberty desirable in itself or only as a means to an end? What are the acceptable constraints on liberty, if any?'

John Stuart Mill answered the latter question with what has come to be known as the Harm Principle: 'The only purpose for which power can rightfully be exercised over any member of a civilised community, against his will, is to prevent harm to others' (*On Liberty*).

The questions raised about liberty and the answers given are clearly relevant to practical politics. Mill's Harm Principle could be invoked, for example, in discussions ranging from the legalisation of drugs to the selection of a whole system of government. In what sense, then, are the philosophers' concerns removed from real-life politics?

The source of the distancing comes from a kind of intellectual division of labour. It is clear that, if one accepts the Harm Principle, there are many questions about how the principle can actually be implemented, or what actually contravenes it. Is it true that drugs only harm the drug user, or do they cause harm to others? What about the harms caused by legal activities, such as gambling or alcohol abuse? It is not that British philosophers have not addressed these issues, but that the mainstream has not tended to address them within the arena of real politics. They have seen their role as working on the general principles themselves and the theoretical resolution of questions that arise when they are applied to particular issues. Translating this into practice or legislation is seen as a task for others.

To a certain extent, this account of the role of the political philosopher is a caricature. In reality, there is a lot of disagreement among philosophers about the relationship between their work and actual politics. But the caricature contains more than a little truth. During much of the twentieth century, British political philosophers did maintain a certain distance from actual politics and at least part of the explanation for that lies in the general, theoretical nature of their deliberations.

This provides the backdrop for the interview with the political philosopher Jonathan Wolff, which investigates this balance between theoretical work and the real politics of the day. The picture that emerges in the discussion is far richer and more complex than the sketch presented by means of its introduction. But the underlying questions are the same. In fact, perhaps there is just one question which informs the whole discussion: what is the role of the political philosopher?

One might expect most people to come to political philosophy through a broader interest in politics, with the philosophical interest coming second. Was that true for you?

I didn't come to political philosophy through active involvement in politics. As a teenager, I grew interested in politics, as a lot of people do at that age, but not in any particularly involved way. I never joined a party or spent time folding leaflets and putting them in envelopes, or anything like that. Looking back, I think I was more interested in moral aspects of the law. The issues which I thought about most when I was younger were to do with punishment and moral sincerity. I remember thinking about the question that if a person really didn't see anything wrong with the way they were acting, how could the rest of us have the right to punish them? That thought doesn't go very far, but that was what I was thinking about.

What happened to me was that I didn't go to university straight away after leaving school. I went to work in the Prudential insurance company legal department for three years. I started taking some of the legal examinations and there were certain things which we briefly covered and I thought were very interesting. It was the philosophical underpinnings of law; for example, questions of rights and duties – do political rights always correlate with duties? Do duties come first and rights come second, or is it the other way around? I talked to the teacher who was pretty sure that I was more suited to the philosophy of law than law. I wasn't very interested in learning Case Law, for example. So he just recommended that I applied to take a philosophy degree.

A lot of people reading political philosophy for the first time expect it to be more politically committed than it is. They would expect to get a very strong flavour of where the author is coming from politically. That's not true of a lot of political philosophy and certainly in a lot of the papers you've published, it's not clear at all what your political commitments are. Some might be surprised by that. What's the explanation?

I've got a general methodological position, which concerns not just political philosophy but philosophy as a whole. Generally, if someone has thought hard and long about an area; if they're intelligent to start with; if they're thinking in depth and if they present a richly articulated body of thought; it's very unlikely that it's all going to be wrong. The most common mistake people make is to have got part of the truth and to think they've got all of it. So my general methodological approach is to be sympathetic to what I read and to try to work out why these people have said what they have said and not to suppose that they're stupid, dishonest or completely misguided. Normally you can find insights in things of all types. I'm very much against the lining up of oppositions that we sometimes see, particularly in political philosophy – putting some people in one camp and others in another and trying to decide which is right. My feeling generally is that there are things of value to be learned in all approaches, and it's difficult trying to fit it all together. In fact, it probably doesn't all fit together. That's why I tend not to pick a firm line and argue it against other people.

If we think about the motivations that people bring to their writing, do you think that people allow their prior political convictions to

drive their political philosophy, rather than letting their philosophy guide them?

That's very interesting. Sometimes people ask what the difference is between political philosophy and political theory. On some views, there isn't any difference between them. But there is a distinction to be made between starting with arguments and seeing where they lead you, and starting with positions and seeing what arguments you can find for them. I tend to think that political theory is more in the latter camp. But political philosophy tries to start at a more general abstract level and to see where it takes you. On the other hand, it does seem to me that there are some good political philosophers who know exactly where they want to end up and just try to find good reasons to get there.

This question relates to the issue of the role of political philosophy. Marx, who has been a philosophical interest of yours, famously remarked that 'the philosophers have only interpreted the world differently, what matters is to change it'. This might appear to be a criticism of philosophers, but it seems to be one that many analytic philosophers would be happy to embrace. How would you respond to the charge that philosophers have interpreted rather than the changed the world?

When he says the point is to change the world, he might not have meant that the point of *philosophy* is to change the world. I think that philosophers ought to be generating ideas that are possible candidates for change. So I don't think that political philosophers ought simply to be interpreting the world. In fact, I don't think political philosophers *are* interpreting the world. Very few of them would claim to be describing the world. Political philosophy is a normative discipline about how the world ought to be rather than about how it is. So political philosophers of all types are putting forward recipes and proposals.

But then there's a question about how much philosophy can achieve. Philosophers might put forward a very general proposal in the way in which, say, John Rawls has done. Rawls' difference principle says that we should make the worst off as well off as we can. That can be a very inspiring political ideal. Some political parties have considered whether they should follow Rawls' difference principle. At some point in the 1980s, I think, the Liberal Democrats had a discussion at their conference about whether they should accept Rawls' principles of justice, but it was voted down on the ground that most people couldn't understand Rawls' writings.

There is obviously going to be a gap between having a very general principle about what ought to be done and its practical implementation. Rawls himself talks about producing principles for a pre-constitutional convention, so that you have these principles, and then you generate the constitution and then you generate laws, particular legislation and so on. Political philosophers shouldn't, I think, be trying to create policy. They don't know how to.

The worry is that the influence in general of political philosophers isn't as great as it should be. Ben Rogers recently wrote in *Prospect*, 'The arguments which Rawls and Dworkin have developed are influential in philosophy but have had little influence on the real world. This should worry them more, I fear, than it does.' And if you look at which thinkers are influencing politics in the UK, it's sociologists like Anthony Giddens and commentators like Will Hutton.

I'm not convinced that either of those are having much immediate effect on what's going on. There's one way in which the rate of political change is very fast – too fast for theorists to have an influence – and there's another way in which it is very slow. Ideas that were coming out of the Chicago school in the late 1960s and 1970s about privatisation, for example, were considered heretical and mad but are dogma now. Things Nozick was saying in the 1970s, and which seemed quite outrageous, became part of the ideology of the mid-1980s.

People used to say the same about Hare and utilitarianism. Hare was arguing for a utilitarian position in moral philosophy, and it might have been thought to have had no influence. But then all you have to do is to stop and think that Whitehall is full of people who studied moral philosophy at Oxford and went to Hare's lectures. Some were influenced by him, and for a time they were all doing cost–benefit analysis, which is a form of utilitarianism.

Now we're not doing so much cost–benefit analysis. Rather we're worrying about who's bearing the cost. If you think about pollution policy now, we don't assert that people can pollute provided there's a greater benefit than harm. We say that the polluter has to pay. In other words, we can't make anyone worse off, and that's far closer to Rawls. So there's a change in philosophical ideas which has come in by the side door, very slowly, and has had an effect on the way we do a certain type of public policy.

It's a kind of intellectual trickle-down theory.

Yes. Dworkin and Rawls teach at elite institutions and the people they teach go into politics and journalism and they do have an effect.

One issue which arises from your articles is the question of what grounds political philosophy morally. Is it a moral theory such as utilitarianism, which you often discuss in your work? Or do you reject the idea that political philosophy should or can have a single moral grounding, in the same way that you reject the view that political obligation has a single source and a single nature?

I think it's a mistake to look for a single ground, thinking you've got to find that before you can do anything else. This is something Joel Feinberg says in his series of four books on the moral limits of criminal law. He says that he hasn't decided which moral theory is the correct one, but that there are plenty of interesting things you can say before you've got to that point. So I don't think you need to have single moral position to get going.

I also think that there's something right about pluralistic approaches. This goes back to the point I was making earlier about great thinkers having rarely got it all wrong. It's quite common to divide up moral philosophy into three distinct traditions; broadly Kantian and duty based; the virtue ethics approach; and utilitarianism. What's interesting to me about the different traditions is that they have a different understanding of what's most morally fundamental about human beings. So in the Kantian tradition, the most important thing is that human beings are creatures with a will who can agree or disagree with certain courses of action – and morality has to take that as basic. In the utilitarian tradition, the most important thing is that human beings and other animals can feel pleasure and pain, so any way of treating them has to take that into account. The virtue-based tradition says what is important about human beings is that they have a good, so things can go well or badly for them, they can flourish or wither. Having these three different approaches lined up, the natural thing to ask is which one is right. But I would prefer to say that they're all true. Human beings have a good, they have interests and they have a will, so any way of treating them has to take all of these things into account. This gives us a complicated, messy theory and might lead us into problems and conflicts, but it doesn't seem to me that we could abandon any of these perspectives. So I do think that for as long as we can keep all of these in play we ought to do that.

I'm also influenced by something the economist Ken Binmore said at a seminar: that philosophers spend a lot of time trying to think about the ideal state of affairs, but they ignore the fact that there are so many ways in which the world, *as it is*, could be made better for everyone. There are so many uncontroversial improvements that could be made, improvements to make everybody better off without making anyone worse off by whatever standard you choose. There are so many ways of doing that, that sometimes it seems unnecessary to get into these controversial arguments where you're reaching for ideals. I don't think that's completely true, but I do think it's a helpful thought that if we can reorganise things without making anyone worse off, then it seems like we ought to do it. What could the possible objection to that be?

In your arguments about competition and libertarianism, there's an interplay between more abstract questions of principle and questions of consequences – what the actual results of these systems will be. In order to make a convincing argument which depends upon consequences, how much do you really need to have a pretty sound grasp of things like, for example, economics, so that you can be sure that the consequences are going to be as you imagine them to be? In other words, how far is it possible to do any kind of political philosophy that is attentive to real-world situations and outcomes without doing a fair amount of social science?

I do think that political philosophy has to be informed by social science, at least to some degree. It may be possible to set out ideals at a very abstract level without making any type of even vague policy proposals and without knowing any social science. But I think that it would be a mistake to shy away from all empirical work. I don't think that this means political philosophers can't do anything without knowing social science, because even social scientists aren't very good at social science – economists often make predictions which don't come true. For example, there was a very interesting debate about the minimum wage, and I was completely taken in by the economists' arguments that if you imposed a minimum wage there would be higher unemployment. In fact, unemployment hasn't increased, and I don't know why it hasn't, at least no more than vaguely. The economy is a very complicated thing, and one can make changes without being sure what the effects of those changes will be.

In addition to your journal writings, you have also written an introduction to political philosophy, which is a very different kind of writing. What motivated you to write that kind of accessible text?

It may sound rather arrogant or peculiar to say this, but I rarely felt able to recommend any of the introductions to political philosophy. The main exception is Kymlica's book, which is excellent but a bit hard and narrow in scope. Raymond Plant's book, which came out not all that long before mine, isn't bad. But the shorter books which were designed for beginners, I found really off-putting. It seemed to me that political philosophy was full of some of the most interesting writing, not just in philosophy, but in culture more generally. You've got figures such as Plato, Hobbes, Mill and they are presenting ideas which are inspiring and in a style of writing which is inspiring. But if you picked up any of these shorter introductions to political philosophy, it would begin with conceptual analysis, trying to define 'authority' or 'the state', going through counter examples, and so on. It was as if they were written with the express desire to turn people off the subject. So I felt a sort of embarrassment for political philosophy that there wasn't something that was more appealing to people, that tried to convey the interest and excitement of the field.

But I don't think it is all that far away from the other types of writing that I do. Although some of it is just a presentation of other people's ideas, most of it does contain ideas which have come from my research in some ways or led to research. Some introductions are referred to as painting by numbers. That's exactly what I wanted to avoid. Rather than saying, here's five pages on something, here's five pages on something else, and so on, I wanted to present a type of theme or argument within each chapter.

Writing the book, the thing that I was keeping in mind at all times was the thought that the reader needs some incentive to turn the page, so there should always be some internal dynamic driving the book, to try to keep the reader involved. A lot of philosophical writing is completely hopeless at doing this. Even philosophical writing for beginners often doesn't do this very well.

Are you interested more generally in writing for a non-specialist audience?

I write for audiences of all levels and even present the same papers at all levels. There are papers I've given to an audience of fifteen-year-olds and at an academic conference – and it's essentially the same paper. I just use longer words on one occasion than on the other. So I think in political philosophy most of the things which can be presented at an academic level can also be presented to intelligent people of any age. The knack of teaching and communicating is just trying to think yourself into the position of the audience. You have to get them interested in what you have to say, on the basis of what they already know. If you can make this empathetic bridge you can explain a lot of things at any level you want. It may take you longer to do it, because you can't build on a shared conceptual understanding, but I think most things in philosophy are capable of being explained, even to beginners.

For a time, libertarianism was a dominant theme in political philosophy, as was communitarianism a little later. What issues do you think are going to be the major preoccupations of political philosophers over the next twenty years or so?

There's a lot of writing about multiculturalism at the moment. That has probably taken over from communitarianism as the hot topic for Ph.D. theses. The discussion of equality bursts into life from time to time and is in a reasonably active phase at the moment, and there's a lot of good writing from people working in that area. One of the things about philosophy at the moment is that, just because there are so many people doing it, nothing seems to go out of fashion any more. There's always going to be someone writing on some area.

To finish, I wanted to ask you about what you're working on at the moment and what you intend to work on for the foreseeable future.

I'm continuing to work on equality. I've been working on disability. What this has brought home to me is the idea that we have to be more sensitive about the issue of rectification of injustice, the rectification of wrong. In a lot of writing, particularly among egalitarians, they take a sort of knee-jerk reaction to injustice that says compensation is required. It betrays a very legalistic understanding of the world, to think that if there is an injustice, a cash payment is what is needed to redress the balance. If you think that people who are disabled suffer in some sense from injustice, then giving a cash payment may not be the most appropriate thing to do. So I think you have to be more sophisticated about forms of redress.

That also maps onto another issue I've been thinking about, which is a debate about the aim of justice. There's one tradition of thought which says that injustice is broadly speaking bad luck, so the aim of a theory of justice is to correct good and bad luck, mainly in the distribution of resources of some sort. We must, on this view, try to even up natural fortune. But there's another view that says that nature is nature, it's not just or unjust, justice is much more about what people do to each other. So justice is about oppression, domination and exploitation and has nothing to do with luck.

This led me to think in my typical fashion that both sides are right and you need a broader picture. The picture I'm working with is the thought that anyone's opportunities to lead a decent and worthwhile life will be determined by two sorts of things. First, there are the resources they have at their disposal, which can include parts of the material world, and also themselves and their abilities, strengths and so on. But also, there's an issue about what you can do with those resources, issues about social structure, in other words. So the particular place you're in – a culture, tradition, society, power relations, the material environment – all these things will affect what you can do with the resources you have. It's often pointed out that people who don't have use of their legs, who have to use wheelchairs, are much better off in a world of ramps rather than steps, or a world of single storey buildings rather than Georgian houses. So you need to take account both of the resources people have and the way the world is configured so they can make use of those resources, both materially and culturally. For example, if it's illegal for people from certain religions to hold certain jobs, or illegal for women to enter some profession or go to university, that's nothing to do directly with the resources of these people, but has to do with the social structures they're part of.

If we find that you lack the opportunities to live the good life that other people have, then that's arguably a form of injustice. But it's not obvious what we should do about it. It seems to me that there are basically three things we might do. One is to change your resource allocation, so the resources you're deficient in are boosted; second, we can leave your resources as they are, but change social structures so that the resources you have are as effective as other people's resources; or third, we can give you a different type of resource, which will enable you to make up for the loss in some way, which is a type of compensation. What I've been trying to argue is that, in general, compensation in that respect is the least useful way of rectifying injustice, even though, as I said, it's the knee-jerk reaction that people have. I want to argue that this relies on a false account of the nature of human well-being, which is roughly that it doesn't matter how you acquire it, as long as you get it. I think it does matter how you get it. So take, for example, cases of women not having a vote. You might say we can just compensate this by giving them more money so they'll achieve the same level of well-being. If you think that's right – as no one actually does – you've got the wrong picture about what's important in human life. How you achieve a level of well-being or success is part of what makes a successful life. That's the picture I'm trying to develop and maybe one day there will be a book on these themes.

Select Bibliography

Why Read Marx Today?, Oxford University Press, 2002
'Levelling down', in *Changes to Democracy: The PSA Yearbook 2000*, edited by
    K. Dowding, J. Hughes and H. Margetts, Macmillan, 2001
The Proper Ambition of Science (edited with Martin Stone), Routledge 2000
Political Thought (edited with Michael Rosen), Oxford University Press 1999
An Introduction to Political Philosophy, Oxford University Press, 1996

4   Aesthetics and Music

In conversation with Aaron Ridley

In the United Kingdom, television at the turn of the millennium has become obsessed with nostalgia programming. We've had series celebrating the 1970s and 1980s, plus a plethora of 'Best Of' and 'Top Ten' programmes, all of which feature music at their centre. One of the interesting things that these programmes show is just how significant music is in our day to day lives. Perhaps this isn't a particularly surprising thought. After all, most of us will be familiar with the sense in which music seems to mark the passage of time. For example, play 10cc's *I'm Not In Love*, and a whole generation of forty-somethings will be transported back to the slow dances of the school discos of their youth. Or, put on a copy of Band Aid's *Do They Know It's Christmas?* and people will think about Live Aid, Wembley Stadium and a hot day in July 1985.

It seems, then, that there is little doubt that music is thoroughly embedded in the social fabric of our lives. What kind of place does it occupy in the philosophical firmament? If it is studied at all, then it is under the remit of aesthetics – broadly speaking, the philosophical study of the arts – which is towards the periphery in the Anglo-American tradition of philosophy. Arthur Danto, a philosopher who has done important work in aesthetics, has joked that the discipline is 'about as low on the scale of philosophical undertakings as bugs are in the chain of being'. Similarly, Aaron Ridley, talking for this interview about aesthetics in British philosophy, notes that whilst it is not considered completely disgraceful to be studying aesthetics, there is no danger that the subject will become compulsory.

What explains the relatively marginal status of aesthetics? This is a difficult question to answer. Partly, it has to do with a feeling that the conceptual space is fairly restricted for a specifically philosophical mode of enquiry when considering issues to do with art. For example, if one wants to understand how music functions both to express emotions and to elicit emotional responses, it seems not unreasonable to think that the most effective tools will be those of experimental psychology. Similarly, if one is interested in exploring the impact of modernism at the beginning of the last century, the best bet might be to do a piece of cultural history or sociology.

On this view, aesthetics is philosophically marginal to the extent that it lacks its own distinctive objects and methods of enquiry. Of course, philosophers will make use of the techniques and research of other disciplines, but they do so at the expense of the *specifically* philosophical character of their own field.

This kind of argument will be contentious. How one responds to it will partly depend on what one sees as being the proper domain of philosophy. The American philosopher Mary Devereaux draws an interesting parallel with the philosophy of science. She points out that reflecting on scientific findings, and thinking about their interpretation and implications, is recognised as an essential part of the job of a philosopher of science. A well grounded empirical knowledge should be seen as a philosophical advantage, not a disadvantage. She concedes that it won't be easy to persuade people that aesthetics is integral to philosophy, but what makes it important is that it is part of a properly philosophical aspiration to understand the nature of human experience.

There is an interesting parallel here between this story about aesthetics and the story that Aaron Ridley tells about the philosophy of music. He argues that music is through and through a part of life. It is thoroughly embedded and thoroughly historical. However, on the whole, it is not treated as such by philosophers. Rather, they prefer to separate music from everything else – to treat it simply as a sound structure – in the hope that it will be possible to establish the pure form of music, an object suitable for philosophical analysis.

However, according to Ridley, the difficulty with this strategy is that it needlessly problematises a whole series of questions that have to be taken seriously by philosophers. For example, it is clear that Barber's *Adagio for Strings* is evocative of melancholy. However, if one is committed to the view that music is just an internally related sequence of sounds, then it isn't clear how one even gets started in offering a distinctively philosophical explanation of this fact. Thus, in Ridley's view, the challenge for the philosophy of music is to move away from the pure sound structure model, and to take seriously the proposition that music is *essentially* culturally and historically embedded.

Am I right in thinking that your realisation that you should study philosophy came as something of an epiphany?

When I was at school, I was a natural sciences and maths kind of person, for reasons which I now never really quite understand. I had a gardening job, and one winter I was out rooting around in the shrubbery, when I had this wonderful moment: I had been thinking of going to university, with a rather heavy heart, and I had hit on geology as being the subject to study. But I had no interest in geology, and I had this moment in the shrubbery when I thought, I don't have to do it at all.

I had been reading generally. I knew that I liked philosophy, but it had never occurred to me that I might study it. And once the penny had dropped, I gave up all thoughts of studying geology with a great sigh of relief. I virtually abandoned my A levels, with nearly catastrophic results, and I squeaked into York to read philosophy.

Once you were at university, were you straightaway interested in the issues surrounding aesthetics?

Actually, the move away from my interest in maths and the natural sciences was rather gradual, so when I first started doing philosophy I was terribly contemptuous of the soft, floppy, artsy side of it. I was terribly keen on logic, the philosophy of science, anything with loads of symbols in it. So for the majority of my undergraduate career, I tended to gravitate towards the more tough-nosed end of things.

And then, of course, the penny began to drop, that what I was actually interested in, what really turned me on about philosophy, wasn't that kind of thing at all. In the background to all this, my main leisure-time interests had always been to do with the arts. I was a fantastically dogged – but entirely giftless – pianist, and a passionate listener to music. So, by the time I graduated, it was clear to me that far from doing geology, or then logic and the philosophy of science, what I really wanted to do was philosophy of art.

So was it as a postgraduate that you first started to look seriously at the philosophy of art?

There was an undergraduate course on aesthetics, but that slightly pre-dated my being serious about the philosophy of art. I thought about doing an undergraduate dissertation on something in aesthetics, but in the end couldn't resist the blandishments of Bradley on the relational form, so I did that. So, yes, I didn't really get serious about it, in any practical sense, until I started my Ph.D.

When you started looking at aesthetics seriously, what kind of image did the subject have among philosophers as a whole?

Well, at York, I think it occupied the kind of place in the curriculum that it would have done in most places. It was perfectly well recognised as being something that was not completely disgraceful, and which it was not irresponsible to have going on in a philosophy degree. But it was never in danger of being made compulsory! And I don't think that anyone would have thought it disastrous if it had proved impossible to put it on for a few years. So it was a bit Cinderella-ish.

How is the philosophy of art viewed now?

There's a famous article by John Passmore, quite old now, called *The Dreariness of Aesthetics*, and I think that for a good while there was this image of aesthetics as being deadly dull. To the extent that it was felt that if it had any life in it at all, it consisted in a minute picking away at the entrails of critical language. So just as during that period you got collections on virtually everything called *X and Language*, so a really significant number of things done in aesthetics in that period were called *Art and Language*, *Language and Art*, *The Languages of Art*, and so on.

And I think that that was on the whole deadly dull. And then, in the 1970s and 1980s, with the rise to some prominence of people like Roger Scruton and Malcolm Budd, aesthetics at last began to get a veneer of non-tedious respectability. But still, you probably find that if a philosopher who is not terribly interested in aesthetics wants a cheap dig, for fun, then it will often be at the expense of woolly minded, namby-pamby, philosophy of art. My colleagues are exemplary in this respect.

It is sometimes claimed that aesthetics can be split into two parts, the philosophy of art and the philosophy of the aesthetic experience and character of objects and phenomena that are not art. Is it possible to make a straightforward distinction between art and not-art?

Well, can I say something first about where I think a more interesting distinction falls in the philosophy of art? It's an issue about where the emphasis falls. Is the emphasis on the word 'philosophy' or is the emphasis on the word 'art'? I think a lot of aesthetics is done with the emphasis on the philosophy, and by that I mean that the motivation or the occasion for thinking about art is prompted by or conducted with the use of conclusions, techniques or methods that have been developed in other parts of philosophy.

This always strikes me as being unsatisfactory, and it is actually characteristic of the majority of aesthetics that is done. It means that the perplexities and problems that are investigated are not raised by the experience of art itself, and then thought about philosophically, but rather the other way around. So I want to see the emphasis as being on art. The art raises the problems, and you want to look at these problems philosophically.

Okay, but what constitutes art, what defines it? I think the question needs to be asked, because, for example, of the suspicion that people have about modern art, where you hear them say it's not really art. Or one could take the example of John Cage's *4′ 33″*, which is a 'musical' composition featuring four minutes and thirty-three seconds of silence. So what defines an object or phenomenon as art?

You're probably going to think that this answer is fantastically evasive, but I've always thought the 'what is art?' question really boring! I don't think that it is an interesting part of the business of being a philosopher of art to give necessary and sufficient conditions for something's counting as art. Or indeed, of being in the business of trying to give clarifications of the sorts of criteria which something might need to meet in order to qualify as art.

The reason why I'm fairly committed to the view that these kinds of questions are boring is that the project of definition seems to me to be a pretty mainstream example of philosophy driving the philosophy of art, rather than the philosophy of art being driven by our interest in objects of aesthetic interest. So, for me, whatever presents itself as being in some way a perplexing object of aesthetic interest will do as a subject for philosophical reflection. In terms of whether this thing is a work of art – well, I don't care.

We are very quick to ascribe aesthetic properties to objects, but I wonder how uncomplicated this process of ascription actually is. Take the notion of beauty – what does it mean when we call an object beautiful?

What's interesting about the notion of beauty is that nowadays, meaning roughly the last century or so, it is hardly ever used. It was really big throughout the eighteenth century – beauty was the primary aesthetic category. But, in the last hundred years or so, it hasn't been so. And one interesting indication of this is that about fifteen years ago, Mary Mothersill wrote a book called *Beauty Restored*, where the idea was to try to bring this concept back into the centre of thinking about art, but I think to no discernible effect whatsoever.

What led to the concept dropping out of aesthetic language?

I think it was a result of philosophy tracking art in a good sense. From the beginning of the twentieth century, there was, in all art forms, a striking fragmentation in whatever had been the prevailing language before that. The effect of this fragmentation was to make it very difficult to think of things in terms of beauty. So, for example, if you look at abstraction in the visual arts, the notion of the beautiful just doesn't seem to be the main category that it's worth employing to characterise these things. Rather, you talk about whether they are stimulating, or thought provoking, or disturbing, something like that.

Part of this has to do with the changing social role that people felt art was performing with the advent of modernism. By the time you hit the twentieth century, art has assumed an overtly critical aspect. And there is an inclination to say that any art that doesn't perform this kind of role is mere entertainment, and this is a view that just couldn't have been held at the end of the eighteenth century.

When we talk about properties like strangeness, do we see them as being more or less universally applicable? In other words, is there a kind of objectivity about these kinds of properties?

If you think 'strange' is a kind of relational property – which it is, things are strange compared to other things – then you have to compare objects with the right kinds of other objects. The strangeness of something can only emerge in an interesting way if it is diverging from the right sort of population, a comparator class.

Given that, it seems to me that there are varying degrees of capacity and expertise in determining what that comparator class consists in. It's possible to illustrate this with a banal example. If I'm listening to some Javanese music, which I don't understand at all, I might very well describe it as strange. All I mean when I say that is that it is not really like music that I'm used to. Somebody who knows Javanese music very well will obviously be in a much better position to pick out any particular piece of Javanese music as being strange. Not because they think the whole lot is strange, but because knowing their way around that idiom, they are able to determine what is unusual or interesting within it.

In terms of universality, I would want to hold on to the thought that amongst people who have acquired an understanding of a particular art form, you'll find very substantial agreement about what is and what isn't strange or interesting.

You've indicated that your particular interest in the philosophy of music emerged out of a general passion for music. What kinds of early interests did you have in the philosophy of music? Were they the standard ones to do with musical expression, representation and so on?

Yes, they were. For the first few years, I was doing philosophy of music with the emphasis on 'philosophy'. So I was looking at the sort of stuff that I later lost interest in. And after a little bit of searching around, it became clear to me that I was most interested in the expression question.

The standard way of setting up this issue is to say that given that music itself feels nothing, and has very few representational capacities – pictorial or linguistic – and yet we have this pretty well entrenched habit of referring to music in emotional terms, hearing music as expressive, being moved by music, and so on, how can this be true? In virtue of what properties is music capable of being expressive or evocative of an emotional state?

This seems like an extremely difficult question for a philosopher to get started on. One wonders why this isn't the domain of a psychologist of music? For example, one explanation for music's expressive or evocative powers would be that human beings have a hard-wired capacity to respond to certain sounds, to certain chord

structures, and they do so, in fairly determined ways. So it's not actually a philosophical issue.

As always with this kind of thing, one has to make a few distinctions. It may, of course, be the case that for some of our attributions of expressive terminology to pieces of music, there is a relatively useful mechanistic story to be told. But this temptation arises primarily when you're talking about the response that one has to the music at a purely emotional level.

But then you think of an example, where the response that one has to a piece of music is real irritation, and you're irritated because you find the music just relentlessly jolly. So what you've got is music being picked out as jolly, but eliciting the opposite of a jolly response.

Couldn't a psychologist say about this, something to the effect that the attribution to the music of jolliness has a hard-wired, causal explanation – there just is something about humans that enables them to attribute jolliness to certain chord structures and rhythms? And that in the case you identify, where you have an irritated response to an attribution of jolliness, this has to do with certain relevant personality and dispositional characteristics?

Wouldn't you think that was a bit of a last resort as an explanation? If one could give an account of why the attribution was intelligible and made sense as a piece of cognition, then there shouldn't be any temptation to think that the best kind of account will be a mechanistic psychological one.

Take a parallel from the philosophy of language. There may well be a lot of things that can be said interestingly by experimental psychology about language use. But you'll never be able to get an interesting answer to the question – what is linguistic meaning? Experimental psychology just isn't going to be able to give a good answer to this question, and I think exactly the same thing applies in the sphere of aesthetics. It's not that psychology is mute in thinking about people's encounters with works of art, or about language, it is just that the sorts of questions that one can reasonably look to psychology to answer aren't the kinds of questions which are philosophically worth pursuing.

In your forthcoming book, you mention that you used to think that the best way to get to the truth about music was to consider it in its pure form. What does it mean to consider music in its pure form, and what's attractive about that way of looking at music?

There's a tradition which is traceable back to about 1800 of thinking that music is essentially just a series of sounds. It seems like a pretty commonsensical assumption. It's gone through various different versions – so, for example, people now often talk about pieces of music as being essentially sound structures. The attraction of this way of looking at things is fairly clear. You're dealing with an object, or a sequence, or a structure of some sort, which is pretty clearly delimited. You can look at it for itself, in isolation from everything else.

This way of looking at music became attractive, non-coincidentally, at the same time as pure instrumental music began to be thought of as the paradigm of music. This happened in the eighteenth century. Prior to this, song, or dance, or Church music would have been much more likely to be offered as a paradigm than music for instruments alone.

The actual historical period during which the majority of important music was written for instruments alone was rather brief. It lasted for about a hundred years, maybe a hundred and fifty years at the outside. But significantly, at the same time, ever more sophisticated techniques for describing music in its purely structural dimension were being developed. These were, in fact, rather scientific conceptions of musical analysis. They dealt with key relations, melodic relations, and so on. And these schemes offered a map or analysis of a piece of music purely in terms of the sounds that it contained or the sonic structures that it comprised.

So, if you put together the rise of a certain sort of music, pure instrumental music, together with the associated rise of some rather powerful techniques for thinking about this kind of music, then there is a strong temptation to think that this is what music essentially is and always has been.

So there's a story about a scientific way of looking at the world to tell here?

Well, maybe it wasn't expressly prompted by any scientistic desires, but there is no question but that certain schools of musical analysis in the nineteenth century and early parts of the twentieth century had explicitly scientific ambitions and a desire to establish themselves on that kind of footing. I think it wouldn't be crazy to say that something of that motivation survives today amongst musicologists and philosophers of music who want to say that music is essentially the kind of thing that is describable by musical analysis.

It's interesting that people place such great emphasis on this quasi-scientific way of looking at music. Take, for example, something like Beethoven's late quartets, particularly, the *Grosse Fuge*. It seems that what is important about this piece of music is not exhausted in the relationships that the notes have to each other, in harmonic and melodic relationships, and so on. What is important is rather its expressiveness, that it expresses some very strong emotions. What kind of response is there to this thought?

To give a broad brush answer, during the heyday of musical analysis the temptation would have been to say roughly what you said earlier, that the emotional dimension is a matter for psychology – that when we talk about pieces of music being expressive, what we're talking about is their effects on us, and this involves some kind of mechanistic, causal story, and is of no interest for the purposes of musical analysis.

If you move away from musicologists, and on to philosophers of music, where this kind of model of music as sound structure is still holding sway, then the philosophical problems that emerge do so precisely because they've listened to something like the *Grosse Fuge*, and they say, 'Yes, it is a sound structure, we're all agreed about that, but it isn't half expressive, and listen to the angst and the torment'.

So the challenge then becomes how an object that you have already characterised as being in essence a pure sound structure can also attract attributions of this sort, or can be heard as having these kinds of properties. And, if you think about the way that this whole question is set up, then you realise that people who want to ask these kinds of questions against a background of a conception of music as pure sound structure, have set themselves an extremely difficult task. They've already conceptualised the object they are investigating in such a way that it cannot intrinsically have these properties.

So what you've tended to find is a series of more or less unconvincing efforts to square the circle. To say, okay, a piece of music is essentially a sound structure, but look, here's a really ingenious way I've got to show that it does nevertheless bear some sort of relation to the extra-musical, that is to say, the emotional. I think that all of these attempts are just bound to look very unconvincing.

From the outside looking in at this kind of thing, it does strike one as almost implausible that this way of conceptualising music, whatever its analytic advantages, became so predominant. I

remember reading about Shostakovich's second quartet, the author was talking about its second movement, and he was telling a story about how the second violin, viola and cello create a backdrop that sounds like it is straight out of a Handel choral piece. On top of this the first violin plays a melody that is explicitly based on traditional Jewish scales. The point is that to understand what's going on here, you have to know that it was written in the Soviet Union in 1944, where anti-Semitism was rife, and that Shostakovich is making an immensely brave statement about compassion and justice. It seems difficult to imagine what a philosopher who buys into a pure sound structure model could say about this?

Well, they couldn't say anything. But I think it is important to draw a distinction here between the pure sound structure model, which with various degrees of explicitness most analytic philosophers have been committed to, and, as it were, the philosophers themselves. In a way, the enterprise has been driven by the attempt to accommodate what everyone knows perfectly well to be the case. So taking your example, I don't think any real-life philosopher of music would dream of saying that all of that biographical, historical, extra-musical information was irrelevant, and therefore that we should turn our backs on it. I don't think anyone sensible has ever wanted to say that.

But the important point is that the pressure within the model that just about everybody accepts is to say just that. And so the philosophical problem is how to say what we want to say without abandoning the model to which we are already committed.

And this presumably is why you think the model is unsustainable as a paradigm of how one should do philosophy of music?

Yes, precisely. How we can take notice of Shostakovich's musical sources in this piece of music only arises as an interesting philosophical problem if we're already committed to a model that makes it look hard to explain. The fact that these sorts of philosophical problems keep arising is, to paraphrase Wittgenstein, the result of the picture holding us captive. That is, the picture of music as being some kind of isolated sound structure. If you're not committed to this picture, then the problems just don't arise in the same way.

So you've moved away from that model, and you now argue that music must be understood as being socially and culturally embedded?

Yes, that's right, woolly as it sounds! I think that if musicologists read this stuff – you know, this whole debate about pure sound structures – then their jaws would drop. They would think that there was something fantastically primitive about the way that philosophers of music see their job. They wouldn't be able to believe we are still thinking in this way. In the 1960s, maybe, but not now. So one way of developing an alternative conception of the philosophy of music would be to try to make some philosophical sense of the commitments and implications of the new musicology, the kind of stuff musicologists have been doing and are doing now, but which philosophers aren't doing. And we're talking here about musicology that does take the context and embeddedness of music seriously.

And this is not a route that philosophers of music want to follow?

No, they've been slow on the uptake and reluctant to follow this path. They'd say that they know that musicologists have been doing this kind of thing, but that it's not respectable and that it doesn't make sense. And so they're going to carry on asking questions that only arise when you juxtapose what you know to be the case with what your theoretical commitments allow you to say. This does strike me as rather a dead-end approach, and I'm trying now to move away from it.

What I'd really like to do, although I haven't a clue whether I'm up to it, is to move from thinking philosophically about the problems that music seems to me to pose, to thinking critically about particular pieces of music. If one's philosophical efforts could end up usefully informing one's efforts at music criticism – though not in the sense of having a critical theory, or anything like that – then I'd finally start to be convinced that the philosophy of music was doing the sort of thing that it really ought to be doing. So watch this space, I suppose.

Select Bibliography

Nietzsche's Conscience: Six Character Studies from the 'Genealogy', Cornell University Press, 1998

R. G. Collingwood: a Philosophy of Art, Orion Books, 1998

'The philosophy of medium-grade art', *British Journal of Aesthetics*, 36: 4, 1996

Music, Value and the Passions, Cornell University Press, 1995

'Tragedy and the tender-hearted', *Philosophy and Literature*, 17: 2, 1993

5   Power, Knowledge and Injustice
In conversation with Miranda Fricker

Epistemology is concerned with the nature, basis and limits of knowledge. One of the central ideas that philosophers utilise when exploring these issues is that there is a difference between holding beliefs for good reasons and holding beliefs – even if they are the same beliefs – for bad or no reasons. This difference is often viewed in normative terms: an individual is correct in believing what it is justified to believe, and incorrect in believing what it is not justified to believe.

The question as to whether one is justified in believing particular truth-claims is not one that concerns only professional philosophers. Rather, it is an issue that people confront every day, and the fact that they do has important philosophical and political implications.

For example, consider the situation where a stranger is asked for directions. What is required for it to be rationally justified that their response is believed? One suggestion is that the informant ought to be believed – that they have *rational authority* – if they are both competent and trustworthy. However, possessing rational authority does not on its own guarantee that the informant will actually be believed. It is also necessary that they are *recognised* as possessing rational authority. And this in turn depends on the presence or absence of certain *markers* or *indicator-properties*. So, for example, in the context of giving directions, a police uniform will likely mark the informant out as someone possessing rational authority, whereas holding a tourist map and sounding confused will not.

The fact that there is a gap between rational authority and its recognition has a number of interesting philosophical and political consequences. In particular, it raises the possibility that whole groups of people might, in certain contexts, have their rational authority undermined, because of the way that markers connect up with patterns of inequality and prejudice. So, for example, the Zina Ordinance, which was instituted in Pakistan in 1979, and which sets out, amongst other things, how rape cases are to be tried in the courts of that country, precludes the testimony of women from counting as evidence, even where it is the testimony of the rape victim herself. And, of course, there are less dramatic examples – perhaps where the complaint of a black person that she is being racially harassed is dismissed, not on evidential grounds, but because 'black people have chips on their shoulders'.

Miranda Fricker has termed this phenomenon, where the relatively powerless are unfairly denied testimonial credibility, *epistemic injustice.* Much of her recent work, and part of this interview, is about this phenomenon and the issues that surround it. However, it is Fricker's contention that epistemic injustice is not exhausted by the case of testimony. It has wider scope.

It is possible to see the social world as being constructed through shared interpretative (or hermeneutical) practices. In simple terms, this just means that social facts – for example, that currencies are mediums of exchange – are constituted in social practice precisely to the extent they are treated as if they are facts of a certain, more or less, fixed kind. The interpretative aspect of this practice comes from the fact that individuals draw upon their understanding of the social world in order to make sense of their experiences, and in order to reproduce the practices that constitute the social world.

A number of interesting thoughts follow from these ideas. There is the possibility that the shared understandings that individuals draw upon in order to make sense of their experience might be more thoroughly shaped by some groups rather than others; and specifically, that it is the powerful that shape the understandings and meanings that are involved in hermeneutical practices. If this is right, then, according to Miranda Fricker, there exists a second kind of epistemic injustice, one that refers to the inability of the less powerful to get a hearing for their social experiences and understandings.

It is the issues surrounding these two kinds of epistemic injustice, particularly as they are informed by feminist theory, that are the focus of this interview, and also of the book which Fricker is currently working on, *Epistemic Injustice: Power and the Ethics of Knowing*.

What originally brought you to philosophy?

My first degree was actually in philosophy and French literature. The two were studied quite separately, and really my first love was much more literature than philosophy. I'm basically interested in people and life – if that doesn't sound too absurd! – and literature allows one to speak directly about such things through a concern with character and story. But I also liked philosophy a great deal, and because I had become interested in feminism, I did an interdisciplinary women's studies MA after my undergraduate degree. It was then, through exposure to feminist writings, that I was first exposed to issues of knowledge, power, authority and social identity – the kinds of epistemology-related themes that I'm still particularly interested in. So mine was a roundabout route back into philosophy. I didn't really feel that it was my own subject until I saw that there could be genuine philosophical topics that concerned issues of power and identity.

Clearly then feminism was very important for your intellectual development. What do you take feminism to be?
I take it in the first instance to be something that I'm too young to have been involved in directly, namely, the political movement for social change that was the second-wave feminism of the late 1960s and 1970s. That's something I've benefited from, and read about, and been inspired by, but not something I took part in.

So was there a recognisable first wave feminism, prior to the feminist movement of the 1960s and 1970s?
Well, there was de Beauvoir writing in the 1940s onwards, and long before that people writing around the time of the French revolution – early radicals like Mary Wollstonecraft and Olympe de Gouges. Actually, it is an important platitude of early feminism that one of its problems is that it rises and falls, rises and falls, and that each wave tends to be forgotten; so that's why it is important to be clear that the feminism of the 1960s and 1970s is (at least) a second wave. Although, it's no doubt inaccurate to suggest that before then there was a single, unified first wave, I think it does make sense to talk about a unified second wave, particularly if one looks at the US and UK.

There is a feeling that this second wave of feminism has lost a lot of the momentum that it built up in the late 1960s and the 1970s. Do you think that the improvements that have occurred for women in terms of educational opportunities, career prospects, and so on, might have something to do with this?
I'm sure that must be right. But there is a difficult balance to be struck

here. I think, in a certain way, academic feminism has got ahead of itself, because issues of equality and freedom are still very real political and practical issues, and feminist philosophy has not done all that much to address them.

I think this is partly because it has exercised its right to discuss what it is most interested in. But also it's significant that academic feminism is hooked into other academic discourses, which, in some cases – certainly in the case of post-structuralism, for instance – became suspicious of these old liberal goals anyway. So there has been an interesting, though in some ways unfortunate, transition in feminist work from a concern with the material to a concern with the symbolic. And although this transition has opened up interesting questions, it has brought a tendency to ignore first-order and material issues.

How does your interest in epistemology tie in with these kinds of first-order issues, if it does at all?

I think it ties in with only one first-order question! My current work starts from the idea that there must be something interesting to say about how power and social identity interconnect with issues of rational authority and the theorisation of knowledge.

Let me give the key example, which is a case of testimony, where one person offers another person a piece of information. Testimony requires that the person who is telling the other person something is both competent and sincere. But there is also a third thing, which becomes obvious when you attempt to theorise the testimonial transaction from the point of view of the enquirer, and that is that it is necessary that the informant is *recognised* by the enquirer as being both competent and sincere.

From that it follows that testimony in a social setting inevitably depends on certain *markers* of competence and sincerity. And the point here is that in the real social world – human societies being what they are – these kinds of markers are likely to be impinged upon by prejudice, with the result that a mere aspect of social identity can cause a person systematically to receive the wrong level of *credibility*. These markers might connect up with accent, for instance – public schools are very good at producing young adults who sound authoritative.

So long as you start with a properly socialised conception of epistemic subjects, then, just theorising something as simple as one person telling another person something can bring to light a general dependence on markers of authority; and it can explain how inequality and prejudice are likely to seep into the question of whether a person's testimony is believed, or how seriously their word is taken.

Let me give a concrete example of this from Harper Lee's novel *To Kill A Mockingbird.* The novel is set in Alabama in the late 1930s. There is a trial of a black man, who has been falsely accused, as the reader knows, of sexually assaulting a woman. It is clear that the all-white jury don't believe his testimony, even though the evidence shows he is telling the truth. So here is an extreme example – from literature, but you can find the same thing in history – of how certain sorts of hatred, prejudice and inequality can actually lead to a situation where a person's testimony is genuinely not believed by a whole group of people who carry authority. The philosophical point being that, at that time in that culture, being black was a marker indicating that you lacked rational authority with respect to certain sorts of issues in certain sorts of context. It deprived you of credibility.

So getting back to your question, this is a first-order issue. What gets revealed here is a special kind of injustice, what I call an epistemic injustice.

You once identified 'traditionalist' and 'reductivist' approaches to epistemology – and you argued that both are limited in certain kinds of ways. What is the significance of this contrast – and what are the limitations of these approaches?

The 'traditionalist' approach to epistemology conceives of the knowing subject as abstractly as possible – sometimes not even as a human being but simply as a rational being, and signally not a being situated in social relations. So the traditionalist does not conceive of epistemic subjects as bearers of social identity, situated in culture and history.

Although there can be excellent reasons for pursuing debates at the highest level of abstraction, proceeding exclusively in this manner does cut off certain lines of enquiry which ought to fit perfectly well within epistemology's remit. Notably questions about how social identity and powerlessness might hinder epistemic functioning – for example, a person's ability to receive the credibility that she, rationally speaking, deserves.

The traditional approach can be contrasted with the 'reductivist' approach, which, in my conception, is a truthful caricature of post-modernist scepticism about the authority of reason. What the reductivist thinks is that there isn't really any special authority that attaches to the force of reason, and that therefore there is no significant difference between rationally persuading someone that *P*, and getting them to believe that *P* by some other powerful means – for example, by their being impressed by the fact that you're some kind of figure of authority.

I think this conception obscures issues of rational authority and injustice just as much as the traditionalist position. The reductivist says something like, 'It's all the same in these games of reason and power; there is no difference between genuine persuasion, and just beating someone over the head to cause them to believe what you say'. The trouble with that is that you can't distinguish between an epistemic practice where people believe roughly what they rationally ought to believe, and one where certain groups are systematically not believed about things they rationally should be believed about. The grounds for distinguishing just and unjust epistemic transactions has been lost with the distinction between rational and irrational ones.

Despite these difficulties with the reductivist approach, which is most closely associated with continental philosophy, there are presumably interesting lessons that traditional analytic approaches to epistemology can learn from the continental tradition?

Absolutely. For instance, I found reading Foucault on power very helpful in thinking about the operation of power within testimonial transactions. There is a big issue in the epistemology of testimony about whether the hearer's responses to the speaker are inferential or not, whether they involve specific judgements. For example, suppose I tell you that it is 4.10 p.m. There's an issue about whether you think: 'Well, this person looks competent, she's looked at her watch, and I've no reason to doubt her sincerity, therefore, I believe her that it is 4.10 p.m'; or whether without any of that sort of explicit judgement, you just believe me. Now I certainly think that there usually aren't explicit judgements going on, and that most cases of testimony are spontaneous and non-inferential. So I take the view that, in the absence of signals to cue suspicion that we're being deceived, we have a certain attitude of 'openness' to the word of others.

But there's more to be said about this, and I think Foucault helps us to see how more must be said about the default of openness. It seems to me that there is always a lot of ongoing social – non-rational as well as rational – interaction when A tells B something. B is not simply standing in a *blank* default position of credulity; rather the degree of

B's credulity is riding on the wave of this social interaction. She is responding to all kinds of social cues – including dubious ones such as accent – as to whether or not her interlocutor seems authoritative. I think we should say there is a *testimonial sensibility* constantly at work, and though I'm happy with the idea that a sensibility delivers judgements of a sort, it will not typically deliver inferences.

So it looks as if the medium in which an exchange takes place is a social medium of power. And the power relations of various kinds that are spurring us on in reacting to one another are intermingled with what is a purely epistemic relation, which is to do with whether or not *in fact* one is rationally justified to believe a person, and whether or not *in fact* the person is competent and sincere. My point is that this pure epistemic conception is absolutely bound up with power relations in that it is only in a power-drenched social context that it can be realised.

Well, this is how I read Foucault's conception of power, and others might disagree. But I think he never tries to collapse other kinds of relationships – knowledge relationships, communicative relationships – into power relationships; rather he says they are always closely intermingled. And I think that's true.

One of the themes running through postmodernism is the idea that the powerful shape our understandings of the world. Is this an insight that feminists have made use of?
Well, the idea that we structure the world, but that that 'we' is not unified and equal – rather disunified and unequal – and that therefore some of us structure public understandings of the world more than others, is originally a Marxist, rather than postmodern, idea. In feminism, *standpoint theory* has taken this basic template, where the concern is exclusively with class, and used it in order to shed light on

gender, and the way in which our understandings of the social world are arguably shaped by men and not women.

I have to say that I think it is unfortunate that a field of feminist theory should have got stuck on a rather moribund grand theory like Marxism, because I think it can hinder fresher engagements in the metaphysics and epistemology of the social world. It is a philosophical commonplace to think that social facts, such as an event being a philosophy lecture, and not a birthday party, say, are not like natural facts, because they are *constructed* whereas natural facts are not, or at least not in the same way. Social facts are peculiarly dependent upon our interpretative, or hermeneutical, practices.

If we allow that the social world is constructed in this sense, and then we add in that the power to participate in those constructive hermeneutical practices might not be distributed equally throughout society, then one has the interesting idea afoot that powerful groups have had a bigger hand in shaping, in really constructing, the social world than less powerful groups.

Whatever one thinks about this, it is separate from the more modest, merely epistemological, idea that our *understandings* of the social world might be more shaped by some groups than others. So one can be more or less extreme about this. Either one goes for the full-on metaphysical view that the very world is constructed in some kind of power-imbalanced way or one can go for the more modest epistemological analogue.

Is your position that there is a matter of fact about social facts, even though they are constructed?

I take the view that the constructedness of social facts is compatible with an epistemic objectivity about whether or not such and such is the case. No doubt there can be very problematic cases, where the hermeneutic practices that constitute the facts are not settled down yet, so that our hermeneutic practice is in some sense in transition. I suppose the difference that I'm evoking then, between social facts that are settled and social facts that are in transition, is a matter of degree. And in terms of our total hermeneutic practice, some aspects of it are going to be extraordinarily entrenched and stable, so we can say with utter confidence that my passing some little metal discs to a man in exchange for a cup of coffee constitutes my *buying* a coffee, whereas we won't be able to say with so much confidence, for example, that a boss's propositioning an employee constituted sexual harassment.

It seems to me that this position is still compatible with a broad realism about social facts. After all, social entities are involved in all sorts of fairly real-sounding things, like causal relations and explanatory relations. For example, the fact that a nation did X caused another nation to do Y in retaliation. Or the fact that my voting explains why such and such a candidate beat her rival in the election. These accounts of what goes on in the social world can stand in all of these very objective sounding causal and explanatory relations, which is an important part of qualifying as real, as it were. But, of course, they're not going to be real in some other senses. The mere fact that social facts have this dependence on our hermeneutical practices does mark them out as different from natural facts. Where one is inclined to draw the metaphysical line depends on how mind-independent one likes one's 'reality' to be. I think it's best policy not to insist on a single line, but to talk instead of different degrees of mind-independence.

Another theme running through your work is, as you put it, 'a necessity for epistemology to accommodate a first-order epistemic pluralism'. What do you take first-order epistemic pluralism to be? Simply the idea that for certain sorts of subject matters, at any given time, there can be more than one equally rational view of the matter. In the case of science, this is obviously perfectly well accepted on the basis of limited evidence, and so on. However, there the expectation tends to be that as more evidence comes in, some of the theories will fall by the wayside, so that there may be convergence among theories. If so, then epistemic pluralism will be short-lived.

But in the case of the social world, where the subject matter is facts-as-constituted-through-hermeneutical-practice, then there is no reason to suppose that there will be convergence, that one picture will emerge. It may be that the right way to understand this is by analogy with a text, something else that is interpretive. Only the most extra-ordinarily positivist readers of a text would insist that at the end of the day there will be a unique, correct interpretation of it, and it seems to me that patches of the social world may be just like this. If so, then any epistemic pluralism in how we interpret, for example, behaviour in the office, or what happened at the board meeting, may well remain indefinitely plural.

How does this tie in with the claim that you made earlier that there is a matter of fact about social facts?
Well, the way the analogy might work is like this: just as the text that permits a plurality of equally good interpretations is itself fixed, so are the social facts that permit different kinds of interpretation.

Of course, in giving our interpretations we are making suggestions about other facts. For example, supposing there is some behaviour that one has witnessed in a boardroom, there are facts that constitute what that is – that there is a certain number of people in the room, that these are their jobs, this was the subject matter, and so on. These facts present themselves as really there and objective because they are very hermeneutically stable. Yet there can still be a plurality of interpretations as to quite why, for example, she got angry with him at that particular time; or about whether or not what happened was some kind of battle of ideologies over the boardroom table, or more a simple clash of personalities. All I need to carry on the analogy between text and social world is that there are some basic secure facts which combine to permit of more than one rational interpretation. All social facts are constructed, yet some are more stable than others; it is at levels of relative instability that pluralism can enter in.

As well as epistemic pluralism, the notion that there are competing epistemic perspectives, you also talk about 'epistemic privilege'. What do you take to be involved in this notion?

I used the notion of 'epistemic privilege' only in a particular paper about standpoint theory, and it is not my own term. What it means is that the standpoint of a certain group – for example, women whose traditional labour is supposed to be relevantly similar to that of the proletariat – gives rise to an epistemically privileged view of the social world.

I reject the idea as it stands, but the grain of truth in it is that having power does tend to make one blind to the ways in which one has power – you notice the distribution of power when you haven't got it. I find this idea very plausible. What worries me is that it's not clear whether it is really something that can be worked into a theory very easily, least of all a general theory about how epistemic privilege relates to powerlessness.

I can only make sense of it by way of the roundabout route that we have, in a sense, been discussing already. And that is to do with how our understandings of the social world have a hermeneutical character, and how participation in hermeneutical practice won't necessarily be even from social group to social group. Instead, the kinds of meanings that are publicly available to us and enacted now, might be prejudicial in that they may be more thoroughly informed by the perspectives of some groups than others. Some such unevenness between men and women might explain, for instance, the slowness to come up with a notion of 'sexual harassment'. What it was like for a woman to be subject to certain behaviours by a man who has power over her was somehow left obscure for a long time, in a way that it surely wouldn't have been left obscure if women, generally, had been more powerful.

That's the only way in which I think that there is a systematic connection between powerlessness and a so-called epistemic privilege. If you want to know how the social world is, you'd better not just look at extant hermeneutical practices, because you should always be asking the question, 'Whose perspective do these understandings represent?' And if you want the full story you had probably better listen especially closely to the accounts of experience that are given by people who are among the least powerful in society. Their hermeneutical disadvantage can become a positive epistemic resource, so long as one can learn to listen. In fact, this is an insight that one finds in deconstruction: some-times the most telling points for interpretation are the 'fractures' in a text – the ways the presented social world *fails* to be coherent.

But isn't the problem with this response that where public under-standings are largely constructed by the more powerful groups in society, it is to be expected that less powerful groups will reflect this fact in the hermeneutical practices that they exhibit?

In very extreme cases of a single ideology dominating collective under-standings, that would be true, and there will be no friction between the experiences of the powerless and collective understandings. But I guess I don't have much truck with the idea of a single dominant ideology –

it seems to be an unfortunately monolithic aspect of the Marxist inheritance. However, if one imagines the kind of situation that you describe, an imaginary Brave New World situation, then yes, you're right, the experiences of the powerless would exactly reflect the hermeneutical practices shaped by the experiences of the powerful. There would be no 'fracture' – yet.

We've been talking about a number of fairly abstract theoretical ideas. Are there practical lessons for feminist practice to be learnt here?

Maybe none! I don't think that it is an obligation on any academic who wants to do work that is informed by feminism or any other political movement that there should be some product that can feedback and make the loop complete. I think the fruits of doing philosophy in a way that is informed by the lived experience of powerlessness are allowed to be simply philosophical. If it gives rise to some worthwhile philosophical ideas that might otherwise be ignored, then that is enough.

However, as it happens, I think some feminist work can have a practical impact. I would personally like to think that ideas about epistemic injustice have a first-order significance that could improve one's awareness of power's operation in discursive exchanges. Certainly, I have found that thinking about these phenomena has made me more aware of such things – their amazing ubiquity. Then there are also ways in which even wholly non first-order feminist philosophy might have wider implications. For example, there is a sense in which it has to be a piece of first-order feminist commitment to stick up for feminist work in a milieu where the very idea of feminist work is received with suspicion or condescension.

Do you have any general views about how philosophy contributes to wider society?

I think that anyone who values culture in general, which I take to include the culture of ideas, is going to value philosophy's contribution to that. And it does seem to me that philosophy offers something distinctive in terms of intellectual style. I think it is a bit ludicrous when people defend philosophy on the grounds that it teaches you how to *think*. That is extraordinarily insulting to other subjects! But there is something distinctive in the abstractness and particular rigour of philosophical style, and in the commitment to any question, any doubt, having a place.

To conclude, perhaps you might like to say something about the situation that feminism finds itself in now. Do you think it is fair to say that we're now in a post-feminist situation?

Well, sometimes I think there is nothing but an unappealing conservatism in the idea of post-feminism. But at other times, when I think about the innocently dismissive reaction of some young women to feminism – which is in fact the most grotesque historical ingratitude, but there we go – I think that there is something real there with a positive aspect to it. It might be considered a relatively healthy reaction against the (wholly unfair) way that feminism became associated in the popular imagination with a psychology of victimhood and complaint. Given that a great deal has been won for women, perhaps there is something optimistic and bold in some younger women's attitude that 'I don't want to make a big deal of being female, I'm just going to go for it and live my life'. Even if there's an element of delusion here, there can also be something positive and life-affirming in this kind of post-feminism. Of course it was feminism proper that made that attitude remotely possible; but maybe a bit of historical ingratitude doesn't matter too much by comparison.

Select Bibliography

'Confidence and irony', in *Morality, Reflection, and Ideology*, edited by E. Harcourt, Oxford University Press, 2000

'Pluralism without postmodernism', in *The Cambridge Companion to Feminism in Philosophy*, edited by M. Fricker and J. Hornsby, Cambridge University Press, 2000

'Epistemic oppression and epistemic privilege', in *Canadian Journal of Philosophy, Supplementary Volume 25, Civilization and Oppression*, edited by C. Wilson, 1999

'Rational authority and social power – towards a truly social epistemology', in *Proceedings of the Aristotelian Society*, 98, 1998

'Intuition and reason', *The Philosophical Quarterly*, 45: 179, 1995

6 Feminism and Pornography

In conversation with Rae Langton

If asked to define pornography, most people would probably talk about sexually explicit films, photographs and books, which are intended to be sexually arousing. However, for many academic feminists, pornography is something very different from this. For example, in *Only Words*, Catharine MacKinnon writes:

> Andrea Dworkin and I have proposed a law against pornography that defines it as graphic sexually explicit materials that subordinate women through pictures or words. . . . This definition includes the harm of what pornography says – its function as defamation or hate speech – but defines it and it alone in terms of what it does – its role as subordination, as sex discrimination.

This definition is highly contentious. Partly this has to do with the fact that it seems to exclude certain kinds of sexually explicit material for no good reason – for example, child pornography involving only males. It also has to do with the worry that the definition is value-laden in such a way that it is a requirement that pornography is seen to be morally objectionable (assuming, that is, that one finds subordination morally objectionable).

There are a number of thoughts that follow from this worry.

Particularly, what kinds of representations, etc., are to be classed as being the sexually explicit subordination of women? Related to this, there is the question of whether there is a space for a separate category, 'erotica', which comprises material that is sexually explicit, but which does not subordinate women.

A second thought has to do with whether or not MacKinnon and Dworkin are right in their contention that the material they classify as pornography subordinates women. This is a matter of considerable complexity and dispute. It depends partly on how one cashes out the notion of 'subordination'. It might be felt that pornography will be obviously subordinating if it can be shown that it leads to an increase in sexual violence. However, it is not agreed that there is any clear-cut evidence that it does have such an effect.

A less contentious claim might be that pornography functions to create and disseminate a constellation of discriminatory attitudes towards women and women's sexuality. Examples of such attitudes might include: that women are defined by their bodies; that their sexuality is exhausted in the desires and inclinations of men; and that they are sexually functional to the extent that they are able to give pleasure to men. If pornography does function in this way, then it is a small step to argue that it contributes to a culture where sexual violence and abuse is likely to be prevalent.

One of the worries voiced about this kind of argument is that it doesn't accord with the positive experience of pornography that some women report. Even if one keeps in mind the definitional point that we're talking here about a certain kind of pornography – perhaps, for example, images of a violent and sadistic nature – there is at least a suspicion that to make any straightforward argument from pornography to subordination is to run the risk of underestimating the complexity of human sexual response and imagination.

Part of the significance of Rae Langton's work in this area is that it shows how one can construct an argument against pornography that does not depend upon the contested empirical fact that it has bad consequences. Rather, what is required is that one shows that pornography – at least, a certain kind of pornography – is an *expression* of misogynistic attitudes. If it is, then the preferences for pornography are sexist, and women have rights against it. This conclusion follows because of a thought common in liberal theory that individuals and groups have rights against the pejorative judgements that other individuals and groups make about their moral worth. In other words, they have rights against 'external', prejudiced preferences.

Whilst Langton shows, with this argument, how it is possible to build a case against pornography that does not depend on a claim about harm, it does not follow that she thinks that pornography has no deleterious effects. Indeed, she takes seriously the claim that pornography has the effect of silencing women in certain sexual contexts. In particular, it is possible that it prevents women from *doing* what they want with their words when they decline a sexual encounter. They might say 'No', and say it loudly, but they are not heard as saying 'No'. If this is right, then pornography subordinates by depriving women of the power to speak without having their words twisted.

It's been interesting hearing from interviewees about the many different ways in which they came to philosophy. What led you into the subject?

I grew up in India, the daughter of missionary parents, and as a teenager I wanted desperately for there to be a clear-cut proof of God's existence. That's how I started reading what I realised later was philosophy. At university, I got into philosophy by accident. The plan was to do English Literature, and I'm afraid philosophy was my fourth choice – I did it because they wouldn't let me do biology! But it gradually came to be what I loved best.

One of the interesting things that has come out of interviewing people for this book is that nearly everyone seems to have got into philosophy by accident.

Yes, it's one of the odd things about philosophy. I can't understand systems like Cambridge where you have to nominate philosophy right from the start. Their students must be people who know themselves much better than average.

When you started studying philosophy formally, what were your first interests?

Sydney University, where I did most of my undergraduate degree, then had two philosophy departments, one broadly analytic and the other broadly continental. I spent time in both of them. And in the department of general philosophy – the continental one – I was keen on the existentialists, particularly Sartre. I wrote an essay on nothingness, which is when I should have realised that I probably belonged in the other, analytic, department, where I ended up, because I was told off for plagiarizing from A. J. Ayer, whom I'd never yet read! Then I became interested in Kant, and in metaphysics more generally. I was interested in realism, and though I never for a moment thought Kant's idealism was right, I found him fascinating. When I decided to study further, I had my sights set on more metaphysics. There wasn't much ethics in my undergraduate career.

So out of those interests how did your interest in feminism emerge?

Well, a significant part of my work still is on Kant and metaphysics. But a feminist political commitment, at any rate, was something that grew over my time in Sydney, partly helped by negative conclusions about God, which made me think afresh about other, misogynistic, aspects of the religious outlook I'd previously taken for granted. Then a philosophical interest in feminism really took off at Princeton. There was a remarkable philosopher and feminist there, Sally Haslanger, who was, and is, an inspiration. And the work you do across a range of topics means you get your toes wet in lots of things you haven't looked at before. That's how it happened.

We were studying Ronald Dworkin, and his liberal political philosophy, and we looked at his article *Do We Have a Right to Pornography?* What struck me was the inconsistency in the view Dworkin was proposing. The nice thing about him is that he takes his starting point to be a principle of equality, that governments should treat the people they govern with equal concern and respect. And, as part of this idea, he thinks we should rule out prejudiced preferences, and that the potential victims of that prejudice have rights protecting them. This is something he is very sensitive to when he considers, for example, issues of racism. So, for instance, he argues that racially discriminatory admission practices are bad because they manifest prejudiced preferences, or 'external' preferences as he calls them; and that blacks therefore have rights against those practices. What the argument hinges on is that the preferences for the racist policy are prejudiced – the preferences wouldn't exist if it weren't for racism. It's not an argument about harm.

However, when it comes to pornography, he never considers whether the preferences of pornographers for pornography might themselves be prejudiced. If he's interested in ruling out these 'external' preferences, then he ought to have raised this question. And such preferences are, arguably, prejudiced. Feminists claim, plausibly, that the preferences for at least some kinds of pornography (and I'm thinking here at least of violent and sadistic pornography) are prejudiced, because such pornography is an expression of a misogynistic attitude towards women.

So what I did in my early article on Dworkin was simply raise for him the question of prejudiced preferences, report his own answer as he had given it with respect to the race case, and then apply that to the issue of pornography. And the conclusion then is that 'we', the pornographers, have no right to pornography, but 'we', the women, do have a right against pornography, because preferences for pornography are sexist. So by Dworkin's own liberal lights, the radical feminist case wins.

So to be clear here, this argument about the right to be protected from prejudiced preferences is not an argument about the harm pornography causes?

That's right. The question as to whether pornography harms is controversial. But you don't need a watertight empirical proof about pornography's bad consequences to get an argument against pornography. The kind of argument I'm offering says, we're not entirely sure what pornography's consequences are, but pornography manifests sexist preferences, and so, in Dworkin's terms, women have rights against it. It's not an argument about the consequences of pornography.

When a consequentialist – someone who is interested in consequences – looks at these issues, am I right to think that they tend to define harm in quite a restricted sense, being to do with whether women are more likely, as a result of the prevalence of pornography, to be subject to sexual abuse, and so on?

Yes. I think what people think of first and foremost where there is a harm argument against pornography is whether or not pornography raises the level of sexual violence or sexual abuse. But there is also a philosophical argument about how this harm is to be understood. When people talk about cigarettes harming people, they talk about them raising the probability that people will get cancer. That's not giving any political interpretation of the harm. But it is different in the case of the harm that pornography is thought to have caused.

Suppose it's true that pornography raises the probability of sexual abuse or violence. If so, that's more than simply harm, it's a violation of women's equality as well, on the feminist argument. Where you have an asymmetric pattern of violence against one group of people, it would be absurd simply to call that harm without recognising the political dimension to it. Here is a class of people who are being harmed in virtue of who they are. So just as you wouldn't say that the lynching of black people was harm without talking about the political dimension, likewise you don't simply talk about sexual violence as harm. You talk about it as an aspect of women's subordination. So the harm argument is interpreted as also an equality argument.

In fact, there is even more to it than this. What you have, especially in the US, is a context where free speech is accorded an almost religious veneration. So pornographer's speech (assuming it is speech), is taken to be worth more than anything else you put on the other side of the scale that has to do with women, whether it is harm, or violations of equality. However, in that context, it makes sense to ask questions about women's own speech. Then you raise the interesting prospect that there might be First Amendment rights on the side of women, not just on the side of pornographers. And so the thought that I've also explored, drawing on MacKinnon, is that the free speech of men silences the speech of women.

This connects with what I was talking about before, to do with how you interpret violence to women. It's not simply about harm, not simply about equality, but also about freedom of speech. One of the ways things go wrong for women is that they might well be able to speak, to say words, but they can't do the things that they want to do with their words – they suffer what I've called *illocutionary disablement*. So, for instance, sexual violence might happen when a woman says 'No', but her word doesn't count as an 'illocutionary' act of refusal.

Although we've been talking about some of the issues surrounding pornography, we haven't yet defined it. This is quite important, I think, because the definition employed by Catharine MacKinnon and Andrea Dworkin, for example, is perhaps not what might be expected. Among other things, it talks about subordination. What are the important issues here?

The most significant part of their definition, as you say, is the part at the beginning: 'We define pornography as the graphic, sexually explicit subordination of women . . .'. That's the part that drew tremendous criticism from philosophers and from courts. You can define something however you want, but there is an issue about whether or not the definition you have matches ordinary usage. In this case, clearly it doesn't. If you look up 'pornography' in the dictionary, you won't find it refers to something that subordinates women. You'll find that it refers to sexually explicit material, designed to be arousing, something like that. So there will be a whole class of things that are sexually explicit and designed to be arousing that don't count as pornography by her definition. She will give them another label, 'erotica'.

So who then decides whether, in any particular instance, there is subordination involved in something claimed to be pornography by MacKinnon's lights?

Well, to decide this, it is obviously not enough that it simply depicts subordination, because there could be material that depicts subordination without subordinating women – documentaries about pornography might do just that. Yes, it is going to be difficult to determine when pornography, as it is ordinarily defined, is pornography in MacKinnon's sense. And there are legitimate worries about misapplication of any legislation. For example, when legislation was passed in Canada, some of the first things that got into trouble were a feminist documentary about pornography, and gay pornography, which I'm sure is the last thing MacKinnon intended. But we can acknowledge the difficulties and still hold on to the idea that her work on pornography is a very significant achievement. I should perhaps emphasise that my main aim has been to defend this understanding from objections that were first and foremost *philosophical.*

What kind of objections did philosophers raise against the definition?

Well, they complained that there is a sleight of hand involved in defining pornography as subordination, to say that it actually *is* subordination. This objection is a mistake. To appreciate why, think about Austin's treatment of speech acts. Austin cared very much about how we do things with words. We utter words that have certain conventional meanings, that's our *locutionary act*, as he put it. Our words have certain effects, that's the *perlocutionary act*. But the central case for him is the *illocutionary act*, that's what the speech act is *in itself.* Once you understand this, and you concede that pornography is speech, you can distinguish between its content, its effect and what it is in itself. Courts often have looked at the content, and asked, does it depict subordination? They have often looked at the effects, and asked, does it perpetuate subordination? But there's still the remaining question of what it is.

MacKinnon's claim is that it is an act of subordination, and I think she is talking about its illocutionary force.

So I think her definition is philosophically defensible. How you decide whether it in fact has that force of subordination is also a partly philosophical question. One thing clear about the nature of illocutionary acts that subordinate is that they can only be done by speakers with authority. That's how an apartheid government subordinates blacks, when it says that blacks are not permitted to vote ('blacks are not permitted to vote' would not be an act of subordination uttered by someone else, say a journalist reporting the situation). Likewise, pornographic speech acts may subordinate women if pornography has authority. So MacKinnon's claim is philosophically defensible, but there is now an empirical part concerning the question of whether pornography in fact has authority. This is something that liberals and feminists disagree about. Liberals like Ronald Dworkin think pornography is a matter of some poor old bloke shuffling around a newsagent, asking for a brown paper wrapper. Women who, one way or another, find themselves inhabiting a pornographic world, and forced to live by its norms, think pornography is the voice of the ruling power.

In your work on speech acts, you argue that pornography as a form of speech might silence women in particular contexts. Is it then because pornography is authoritative that it has that power?

That's a good question. And the simple answer is yes, but it's not the whole answer. I probably wasn't entirely clear about this in 'Speech acts and unspeakable acts'. I was exploring two claims: that pornography subordinates, and that pornography silences. Both these claims were understood in speech-act terms. Pornography subordinates because it ranks women as inferior and deprives them of certain powers. That is part of the story. This then connects with the second claim, because among the powers that it deprives women of is the power to speak without having their words twisted – the power to say 'No' and mean a refusal by those words. This is the idea that pornography helps create illocutionary disablement. Understood like this, the silencing claim is part of the subordination claim. So, if pornography subordinates authoritatively, and if it subordinates in the way that I describe, then it silences women by virtue of its authority.

However, one thing that is possible, which I didn't explore there, is that pornography may silence women whether or not it is an illocutionary act of subordination. That is, it might simply be a matter of its causal consequences, as a perlocutionary act. It might change the beliefs and desires of men, and alter the conversational circumstances that men and women inhabit so that as a matter of causal fact, women encounter illocutionary disablement, they are unable to say what they intend to say. Jennifer Hornsby might perhaps view things more this way, she would say that pornography undermines the 'reciprocity' that is a condition of successful communication. Pornography might do this, not because it is particularly authoritative, but just because it is a causally potent social phenomenon.

How did you argue for the authority of pornography?

It is not an easy question. What I talked about was the size and power of the pornography industry. I also talked about the way in which it is held to be an authority on matters of sex by a large number of its readers. People's beliefs and desires are changed on exposure to certain kinds of pornography, that's fairly clear empirically. They are more likely to view women as inferiors. They are more likely to think that a rape victim had deserved to be raped. They are more likely to favour a lenient sentence for the rapist. These sorts of things have been fairly well documented in laboratory settings.

So we have some effects. Now we don't here want to use these effects directly as part of the philosophical argument. It's not simply a harm argument. So we ask: what's the best explanation of those effects? And I suggested that a good explanation is that the readers are regarding pornography as authoritative, otherwise they wouldn't change their beliefs.

So is your argument that pornography has certain effects, which suggests that it is authoritative, and because it has the authority, plus the effects, you can then make an argument that it subordinates?

Yes, that is certainly part of it. I think it is pretty well documented that pornography alters people's beliefs. Incidentally, that raises an interesting question about how something presented as mere fiction can possibly change people's beliefs. On the face of it, there is something very peculiar about it. To take an old example everyone knows about, think of what happened when the film *Deep Throat* went on to the market. It was a film starring Linda Lovelace, and it had a science fiction premise that Linda Lovelace had a clitoris in her throat – the story only made sense on the assumption of that science fiction premise. The extraordinary thing is that it altered people's sexual practices. Presumably it didn't alter men's beliefs about the truth of that fictional premise! But it apparently altered their beliefs about what some women would find arousing, and certainly it altered their beliefs about what some men would find arousing. So there is something peculiar about the way that pornography alters people's mental states, even though it is fictional. The example suggests we should perhaps be looking at irrational desire change, rather than simply belief change.

But if it didn't alter people's beliefs and desires, despite having the same locutionary force – so, in this example, you still have Linda Lovelace, and the same story – would the argument to subordination then be much harder?

It might suggest that pornography didn't have the sort of authority feminists were ascribing to it. Of course, there could in principle be authoritative speech without that speech having distinctive effects. But yes, you'd be deprived of some of the evidence that subordinating speech was going on.

So it seems to be the case that the force of your argument rests on the presence of empirical facts about the way that pornography changes people's beliefs and desires. Are you confident about the empirical evidence?

The argument that pornography subordinates, you mean? Yes, as I said, I think it is fairly well established that pornography has at least the effect of changing people's beliefs and desires, and that helps support the premise about authority. I'm thinking here of evidence cited by social scientists – such as in Edward Donnerstein's *The Question of Pornography*. This question is distinct from evidence to do with harm, where that is understood as actual violence. You don't have to look at this sort of harm to answer the question about whether pornography is authoritative. However, if you are also going to argue that pornography silences, that it prevents women from being able to perform illocutionary acts of their own, that argument depends on a different empirical claim again, namely that women get their speech acts twisted in certain sexual contexts.

It might be interesting to explore very briefly some of the implications of your argument about speech-acts and illocutionary disablement. If a woman's illocutionary act doesn't achieve uptake, that is, she is unable to say what she intends to say, then in those date-rape cases where the accused says that they thought the woman had said 'Yes', even though she actually said 'No', they might be telling the truth? Is that a worry?

Surely a first point to make is that a necessary condition for consent is that you intend to consent. So, whatever the case, the woman in your example hasn't actually consented. Now your point is that he believes she consented. And he believes with what he takes to be good evidence that she consented. And you're perhaps worried that he would there-fore not be guilty of rape, or at any rate that he has extenuating circum-stances. If what you're describing were so, we'd have something chill-ingly similar to stories told at the Morgan rape case back in 1976. Morgan was a man who invited three of his friends home from the pub to have sex with his wife. He said that she would put up a fight, but she liked it a bit rough. The three men came home with him, and she did indeed put up a fight, and said 'No', but was raped. The question that arose out of that trial was, roughly, whether or not the defendants were guilty of rape, given that Morgan had said resistance counted as con-sent for her. Actually, the jury didn't believe that the men believed she was consenting. So the men were sent to jail. But there's the hypo-thetical question – suppose, on the basis of what Morgan had said, they had believed she consented? That then parallels what you are suggest-ing: suppose these men falsely believe, on the basis of what some pornography tells them, that the woman they raped was consenting?

The hypothetical question is what made the Morgan case so con-troversial. What the majority of Law Lords said at the time was that if the men honestly (even if unreasonably) believed it, they wouldn't have been guilty. This provoked a great uproar, with many rightly saying this was a charter for rapists. It has since been said that belief in consent is not a good enough excuse, though reasonable belief might be. But look, the sad thing about pornography, on this way of thinking, is that it really does sometimes distort communication in sexual contexts. This doesn't undermine the responsibility of people to get the communication side of things right. I don't think blaming pornography means that you therefore don't blame individual rapists. And yes, I can see how the issue comes up.

But whatever we think of this, let's not forget Morgan himself, who parallels the pornographer of your example. His lying words to his friends about his wife were speech, 'only words' you might say – 'Only Words' was the title of MacKinnon's recent book – but were they therefore innocent? No. And if that's what we think about Morgan, perhaps that is what we should think about pornography.

I believe that you are still working on some of these kinds of issues. In what kinds of direction are you taking this work?

Well, besides arguing against pornography, MacKinnon has also argued against philosophy itself. She talks about certain ideals of objectivity, certain epistemological standpoints, as being the basis of objectification. To put it in a sloganeering way, she says that objectivity objectifies.

Now I'm a philosopher, and a feminist, and therefore tend to think objectivity good, and objectification bad. So it would be sorry news for me if she were simply right, and objectivity turned out to objectify women. But MacKinnon is a challenging thinker, so I've been exploring this question in feminist epistemology of what connections there might be between objectivity and objectification.

Objectivity is, in part, about how your beliefs fit the world. It has, so to speak, a certain direction of fit. Your beliefs ought to fit the world, not the other way around. Objectification has the opposite direction of fit. It has to do with how the social world, the world of women, comes to fit the world of men's beliefs and desires, and, more generally, their mental states. So there's a very different direction of fit. And what might be right about what MacKinnon says is that not objectivity, but a certain *assumption* of objectivity, might help to objectify.

The thought goes like this, building on some work by Sally Haslanger: Suppose objectivity is just assumed – people assume that their beliefs have the normal direction of fit, assume they fit the world. Really what is going on is a process of objectification, which is in certain ways akin to wishful thinking and self-fulfilling belief. With wishful thinking, you have belief fitting desire, rather than belief fitting the world; with self-fulfilling belief, you have the world coming to fit belief, rather than belief fitting the world. With objectification, men desire women to be a certain way, and that makes them believe they *are* that way, as with wishful thinking – a process which could well be aided by pornography. In situations of gender hierarchy, such beliefs can become self-fulfilling: women get shaped by how men think and believe and desire. That is part of what objectification is. And if, while this goes on, men assume they're being as objective as possible, all these objectifying mechanisms will be disguised. That's part of the sense in which MacKinnon may be right. The assumption of objectivity can mask and disguise objectification, and help perpetuate it.

This sort of exploration takes things deeper philosophically than just sifting through empirical issues about what's been done in a particular lab with students exposed to pornography. And I think, by the way, you don't have to be trained in any esoteric theory to grasp what is at issue here, or assess its plausibility. This brings us again to that issue of *communication* which has been running right through our conversation – whether it's sexual communication we're talking of, and pornography's disruption of it; or whether it's communication between academic feminists and philosophers.

Connecting these philosophical and feminist issues in another way, I'm also curious about the analogy – if it is a mere analogy – between the solipsism of Descartes' lonely meditator, and the sexual solipsism of pornography. The meditator imagines he's the only person, he sees as mere automata the creatures in hats and coats outside his window, he views those people as things. Does the pornographer likewise view women as things? That's a topic of a book I'm writing now.

Select Bibliography

Kantian Humility: Our Ignorance of Things in Themselves, Oxford University Press, 1998

'Free speech and illocution' (with Jennifer Hornsby), *Legal Theory*, 4, 1998

'Pornography, speech acts and silence' in *Ethics in Practice*, edited by H. LaFollette, Blackwell, 1997

'Speech acts and unspeakable acts', *Philosophy and Public Affairs*, 22: 4, 1993

'Whose right? Ronald Dworkin, women, and pornographers', *Philosophy and Public Affairs*, 19: 4, 1990

7 Mind Matters

In conversation with Tim Crane

The philosophy of mind was one of the most important topics in British philosophy in the twentieth century, and it shows no signs of losing its pre-eminent role as we begin the twenty-first. Perhaps one reason for this is that several things can all appear to be obviously true about minds which, nonetheless, can't all be true since they contradict one another.

Take a popular line of thought that can be traced back to Descartes. If we consider what matter is, we can come up with a basic list of its properties: it is extended, it has mass and shape and is subject to physical laws, such as those governing cause and effect. Now consider mind. This does not appear to have the same kind of properties at all. Thoughts cannot be measured in nanometres. Ideas don't have physical weight or occupy space. And it is not gravity which brings speculative thoughts down to earth. Therefore, it would seem that mind and matter have very different properties, so, whatever mind is, many have been convinced that it must be a different kind of thing to matter.

The compressed argument presented here is obviously crude, but versions of it and the theory we end up with – dualism – have appealed to many philosophers and non-philosophers. Many find the idea that mind is a different kind of thing to matter very appealing, if not intuitively obvious.

But a different line of thought leads to a different conclusion. We know that the brain is what makes consciousness possible. We know that if you change the biochemistry of the brain, by taking a hallucinogenic drug, for example, you change what thoughts are had. We know that if the brain is damaged in specific regions, specific functions of mind are lost or impaired. In short, surely we know that whatever the mind is, it is a function of physical brains.

This might lead us to a view which conflicts with dualism. Rather than thinking of mind and matter as two different things, we might take a monist view and claim that there is just one thing. In particular, we might think that this one thing is physical, since it is the existence of the brain which we take to be fundamental, and brains are physical entities.

These two views conflict, and an enduring problem in the philosophy of mind has been to see how each can do justice to what seems obviously true in the other. For example, how can the dualist account for the 'obviously true' fact that brain functioning is essential for mind functioning? If mind and matter are completely different, how do we account for the intimate interaction between the two?

On the other hand, how can the physicalist account for the 'obviously true' fact that thoughts, feelings and so on are not things which have physical properties of weight, mass and size? If matter is all there is, how can there be thoughts at all? Thoughts just aren't a part of the physical description of reality.

Given that both dualism and physicalism seem to offer obviously true accounts of mind and matter, yet both can't be true, it must be the case that some of what seems obviously true is actually false. To resolve the difficulty, we need to move beyond the straight dualism/physicalism debate to examine a range of concepts and notions in the philosophy of mind, which together can paint a richer picture than that offered by this old opposition.

Tim Crane's work in the philosophy of mind has focused on some of these other issues. In particular, he has worked on the ideas of representation and intentionality: the ideas that mind represents the world and that thoughts are about things in the world. Considering these two features of mind is both an intriguing and worthwhile philosophical project in itself, and a means of gaining a different, fresher perspective on the apparently intractable, and sometimes stale, debate between dualism and physicalism.

How did you first come to philosophy?

I think I came into philosophy through my interest in religious questions. That's quite a common route, I think. I was brought up a Catholic, which was an important aspect of my youth. Through those questions, I started getting interested in questions about the meaning of life, the nature of the world and transcendental questions about the existence of God, life after death and so on.

What age were you when that started translating into a reading of philosophy?

I must have been about sixteen or seventeen. I studied religious studies at school for A level and this involved quite an intensive study of the Bible, from a historical perspective. That raised many questions in my mind about how exactly you were supposed to read this text and whether it was possible to interpret it not as trying to express the literal truth, but rather as trying to express some other kind of truth. I was attracted to this idea of other kinds of truth. Now, of course, I'm not interested in that idea at all.

Those interests are quite far from contemporary philosophy of mind, though not entirely separate from them. So how did you end up focusing on the philosophy of mind?

One of my teachers recommended a book edited by Andrew Woodfield, called *Thought and Object*, and told me this was the most interesting book that he had read. It was a collection of essays on the subject of the content of thought. I was captivated by this idea, and I wanted to learn more about it. And, in a way, I suppose I've stayed with it.

It's interesting that in the case of several of our interviewees, what first attracted them in philosophy ended up being their special-isms. Does that say anything about how people are trained in philosophy – that it's quite easy to end up sticking with what first grabs you?

I think there is something which could perhaps be a danger, which is excessive specialisation. In order to make progress and in order to make your ideas public, you have to focus on something very specific and say something original about that. That means that the old idea of the general philosopher, someone who could say a little about everything, and publish papers on a variety of subjects, is to some extent less common than it was. I'd prefer to be that kind of philosopher, but I've ended up a rather specialised one.

As a graduate student, you spent a year in Wisconsin, where the dominant figures and movements in the philosophy of mind were different to those in the UK. When you go to a university in a country like the United States, where the philosophical tradition is not so distant from British philosophy, but you see that the whole canon is different, how does that affect the confidence you have that the subject is developing on a secure basis? Doesn't it raise the

possibility that there's a certain arbitrariness in who and what is seen as important?

For me it opened my mind. For the last fifty years, I think there's been a danger in British philosophy of being very closed-minded, though that's less the case now. The other thing is that it makes you think about philosophy itself and what kind of enterprise it is. There are certain different ways of doing it. This is one of the things that distinguishes philosophy from science. You don't just have disagreement about particular issues, you have disagreement about the nature of the subject. Two people could disagree about their theories of mind, and there could be someone else, in the same academic department, the same discipline, who thinks that this is completely the wrong way to address questions of mind, and other people, even within philosophy, who think philosophy is at an end. The extent of the disagreement and its foundational character can't be seen as accidental or an unfortunate inadequacy which will eventually get ironed out.

If you take that as being central to the very nature of the subject, how should that inform the way we view the theories and arguments we put forward, knowing that one could reject the most basic premises we need to get going?

That's a really hard question about the methodology and epistemology of philosophy. My feeling is that you shouldn't really be expected to convince people, but you should be able to convince yourself that you've said as much as you can, as clearly as you can, and that in so far as your position has inadequacies, you know what they are and you think that they are less bad than the inadequacies of other positions. That's a bit defensive, but in a way philosophy is an individual enterprise – you try to describe things as you see them and then tell them to the world. Whether the world listens is not within your power.

The question of whether the world listens leads on to your book *The Mechanical Mind*, which is aimed at a broad audience. At the same time, it is quite meaty, dealing with substantial issues, though it doesn't say anything that couldn't be followed by someone with sufficient intellectual resources, even if they hadn't had any special training. How far do you think you can take that kind of writing? Obviously, there are ways in which you have to draw lines around things and say 'this takes us beyond the scope of this book', but you have to do that in academic writing too. So how much of what could be said about the philosophy of mind could be written in the style of *The Mechanical Mind*?

I'd like to think a lot more than currently is. Partly due to the number of people writing in this area, everyone wants to carve out a little space for themselves, so a lot of people make things spuriously technical. There's a lot of scholasticism in the subject. Often people lose the sense of what is significant and what isn't. In the subject of my next book, the philosophy of consciousness, there are lots of issues where people get hooked on certain ways of talking and describing things.

That's an interesting point because it could be said that one reason to adopt a technical vocabulary is economy, that you can say things much more quickly if you don't have to explain all the terms you're using. But then I thought one of the interesting things in *The Mechanical Mind* was that in explaining the vocabulary you were actually bringing to light things that were unsatisfactory about the way in which the various terms and concepts were used. So in having to explain what they meant, you brought out the fact that people were using a technical vocabulary without questioning the assumptions that lie behind it.

I agree with that. One of the things I wanted to address in writing *The*

Mechanical Mind was that I felt that there wasn't a book that explained to people who didn't have knowledge of computers, what it meant to say that the mind was a computer. A lot of books, even introductions, seemed to assume that people knew what a computer was, or a Turing machine, without telling them who Turing was and what his machines were. That was one of my aims. Another aim was to clarify terminology that wasn't itself clear. I agree with you that all philosophy should be foundational in the sense that you have to be absolutely clear what it is that you're taking for granted or else you end up with debates that are going nowhere.

One issue that has dominated the philosophy of mind has been the issue of physicalism. Could you briefly explain what is involved in the notion of physicalism?

I suppose that every student knows that Descartes was a dualist – he thought that mind and body were distinct things. One way of denying dualism is to say that mind and body are not distinct because mind is a physical thing. For example, mind is the brain. Physicalism is a modern version of such a view. The term physicalism goes back to the philosophers of the Vienna circle in the 1920s. Physicalism, rather than the view that everything is material, is the view that everything is physical, where being physical is being the subject matter of physical science, which is supposed to be the science that has told us most about the general nature of the world. All other sciences are known as special sciences, because they tell us things about particular areas of study, whereas physics of its nature has application to everything.

So physicalism could be understood as the view that everything is physical. But if that means that everything is the subject matter of physical science, then it's ambiguous. On the one hand, you could mean that everything is subject to physical laws, which is just to say that physical laws are general. That's an unexceptional doctrine. But there's also the view that the only things that there are, are the things that physics talks about – atoms, molecules, electrons, forces, fields and their properties. That is a view that very few people take. At that extreme, physicalism is not a tenable view.

Many philosophers think that we should believe in something called non-reductive physicalism, which says that everything is subject to physical laws, but that certain things cannot be reduced to the things talked about in physical science. Non-reductive physicalists say that the mind, and mental properties and features, are the *properties* of something physical but are not *reducible* to physical properties or features. It seems to me that this view shouldn't say that everything is physical, but that some things are physical and some aren't – and that's my view. Having said that, it seems that there's not much point in calling yourself a physicalist, because then you're really a kind of dualist, or as I would prefer to say, a kind of pluralist – there are many kinds of things, some of them are physical in this narrow sense and some of them aren't.

Is it correct to say that you think the philosophy of mind has been too concerned with the debate over whether physicalism is true and that where one stands on a lot of issues in the subject does not depend on where you fall in that debate as much as is usually thought?

Consciousness is an example of this. Suppose there are these two views, physicalism and property dualism. Reductive physicalism says that consciousness is a brain state. Property dualism says that consciousness is a property of the brain, but not a physical property. Now you might think that this is a very important dispute, and it is important in some ways. But it's not important when it comes to the traditional philosophical problem of understanding what consciousness is. It doesn't tell us anything about what distinguishes the conscious from the unconscious, and it doesn't help solve traditional philosophical issues about the relationship between consciousness and intentionality or mental representation, for example. So it seems to me that whatever line you took on whether consciousness is physical or not, you'd still need to have a theory of consciousness and that's what I'm interested in.

The philosopher Hugh Mellor and I made a joke, which no-one found particularly amusing apart from us, which is, suppose that all flesh is grass. Even if that's true that doesn't explain the difference between vegetarians and non-vegetarians. Vegetarians think that some grass is not okay to eat, but other grass is.

So the point is that the problem of consciousness is the problem of how stuff can be conscious. Whether that stuff is physical or not, doesn't give you a direct answer to that question. So the idea is that there are general problems that need to be solved prior to more particular disagreements between theories. This links up with some of what you say in *The Mechanical Mind*. There you say that there is a general problem of representation, which needs to be dealt with before you even get to the specific problems of representation in the philosophy of mind. What is that general problem?

It's one of those things that seems to me intrinsically puzzling once you start to think about it – how can anything represent anything at all? Take any simple representation, such as a word or a picture, and look at the word or picture and think, how can that come to mean what it does? How can it come to stand for what it does? The initial answers that one is tempted to give are always unsatisfactory. You could say it's a convention or it's associated with an idea in your mind or it's part of a human linguistic practice – these are just gestures towards a theory. If you look at a word, it looks so familiar and seems to carry its meaning with it, but it's just a physical object, just marks on a page.

One thing you take from Wittgenstein is the idea that he came to reject, that something might represent something else because it resembles it, and he takes the example of a picture of a man climbing up a hill. Why can't that represent a man climbing up a hill?

Wittgenstein encourages you to look at something like that and ask what it is about that picture that makes you think it's a picture of a man climbing, rather than a picture of a man sliding down a hill.

How does this general problem of representation relate to particular problems of representation in the philosophy of mind?

It's one way into some of the main problem areas in the philosophy of mind. The general problem about representation is such a striking and gripping thought, which should then influence your initial attempts to explain that problem in terms of what the mind does with these representations. What does the mind do? It represents. It uses certain things to represent other things, which pushes the question back into the mind. You need a way of understanding how the mind represents. In *The Mechanical Mind*, I assume that mental representation is the most fundamental form of representation, because without it representation generally would not be possible – that's a fairly orthodox assumption. The main part of the book expounds the view that we can understand aspects of how the mind represents by taking seriously the view that the mind has a computational structure. Those are ideas that come from Fodor. But, in the end, it seems to me the computational theory of mind leaves us no further forward when we're talking about the original problem of how anything can represent at all. After all you're just saying how do the symbols in the computer, your brain, represent?

This relates to the issue of intentionality. This is a question which a lot of people find difficult, perhaps for the simple reason that it is often misdescribed. How is intentionality usually characterised?

The term intentionality is a technical one, which goes back to the Middle Ages. Certain medieval philosophers used the word '*intentio*' as a term for 'concept' or 'idea'. This terminology was picked up again in the late nineteenth century by the German philosopher Brentano. Brentano claimed that all mental phenomena had this property of intentionality. Brentano used the term intentional to apply to states of mind which have objects – they're about or directed on particular things. This is easily understood in certain cases: If you're thinking, you're thinking about something; if you believe, you believe something; if you want, you want something; if you dream, you dream of something; if you see, you see something. That is the feature of mental states which is picked out by the term 'intentionality', that for each state of mind it must have an object. There must be something it is about or directed towards.

There's a fair amount of disagreement about how far this is a defining mark of the mental, but to a lesser or greater extent, people have to accept that there is intentionality. But how does representation relate to intentionality?

Some philosophers use the word intentionality just to mean mental representation. I think that can be a bit misleading, if you take seriously what Brentano said – which was that intentionality is the mind's direction on its objects. He thought that all mental phenomena involve that direction on an object. Many philosophers these days reject that on the grounds that there are mental phenomena which don't involve a direction on an object, for example, bodily sensations. If you've got a pain in your leg, it's not about anything.

I think this is an interesting question because, after all, Brentano was presumably aware of the existence of sensations, so what did he have in mind when he said that all mental phenomena, including sensations, were intentional?

The way to answer that question, I think, is to try to separate out the concepts of intentionality and representation. If intentionality is a matter of a state having an object, then a sensation can be thought of in that way. You could say, for example, that a pain in your leg is something that seems to be in your leg. So I would say that your leg then should be thought of as the object of your state of mind. So there is a directedness on an object, it's a directedness on your leg. However, you could say that, without saying that your mind represents your leg. It's rather that your mind apprehends your leg and that the leg is the object of your state of mind. Some people have said that pains represent damage to the body. I don't think that's obvious and we don't need to believe that to believe that states of mind are intentional.

So I think we can separate out the ideas of intentionality and representation because, after all, the idea of representation goes along with the idea of correct and incorrect representation. In the case of a pain in your leg, what does it mean to say that the pain is correct or incorrect?

To get some idea of what's at stake in these debates, in one of your papers you pick up a quote from the American philosopher Richard Rorty, where he says that pains and beliefs are both thought of as mental yet have nothing in common except our refusal to call them physical. This is a fascinating question, because it suggests that the

philosophy of mind is being done without a clear idea of what the mental is. So part of the importance of talking about intentionality, representation and consciousness is trying to pin down what is meant by the mental. Is there a question of whether there is a genuine single category of the mental in the first place?

That is an important question, because I do think that we have a distinction between those things which we think of as subjects of experience, subjects of thought, and those things that we don't. I think a philosophy of mind ought to understand that distinction. Of course, that distinction may be blurred at the edges and we may not be able to say of a certain kind of creature whether it's a subject of experience or not. I think at the heart of it is the idea that subjects of experience or thought are those that have a world, which is a traditional phenomenological idea. In Nagel's phrase, there is something it is like to be a subject of experience. There is something it is like to be a goat, I think, but there isn't a something it is like to be a table. This is the distinction we're trying to mark.

If you try to say what that is in terms of the traditional distinction between intentional states and conscious states, you'd ask whether that thing having a world is supposed to be a matter of intentionality or a matter of the conscious, qualitative nature of states of mind. It's clear that it's both. If I say what the world is for me, I start describing my environment, but as it appears to me, consciously. But that's also describing the objects of my states of mind. So it seems to me intentionality and consciousness are inextricably linked when it comes to saying what it is for something to have a mind.

You don't think that the idea of consciousness captures all that we want to put in the category of the mental?

No. I don't think it does. I think you have to make room for the idea of unconscious mentality. Whether or not there could be a creature whose mentality is entirely unconscious is not something that I have a fixed view about. But I think that our primary use of the idea of mentality is in the case of conscious intentionality.

We've been talking about some of the issues that have concerned you in the recent past. What do you think will be the most pressing issues in the philosophy of mind over the next ten to twenty years?
I think that the 1970s was the decade of the theory of meaning, the 1980s was the decade of the theory of mental content or mental representation, the 1990s seems to have been the decade of consciousness. For myself, I think the questions around the relationship between mind and actions are still not as central as they should be. A lot of philosophy of mind works on the assumption that the relationship between mental states and events and actions is a relatively straightforward causal relation. So you go from mental states, conceived in terms of beliefs and desires, causing actions, without any ineliminable role for ideas such as intention, decision, reflection and practical reasoning. Practical reasoning, intention and decision, and so on are discussed, but almost as a separate area of philosophy. I would be interested in seeing how this could be integrated into the mainstream of the philosophy of mind. It's something I'm interested in finding out about. It also leads into very difficult issues concerning the freedom of the will, which is in the background of a lot of these discussions about reductionism and so on. Even some non-reductive philosophers don't want to face up to the consequences of their views for freedom of the will.

What are you personally going to be working on?
I'm working on a book called *Elements of Mind*. I'm trying to break down the distinction between intentional mental states and the

non-intentional or qualitative mental states. I want to defend Brentano's view that all mental states are intentional. The way I want to do it is by an examination of the main areas of mind: thought, consciousness and perception. It's different from my previous book in that I'm not really addressing the question of whether there can be a reduction of intentionality to representation because it seems to me clear from recent investigations that there's not much future in that view. It's the sort of thing you could carry on for the rest of your life, but I'd quite like to do something a little bit different from the philosophy of mind. I'm interested in very traditional questions of metaphysics and epistemology, and I'm also interested in the recent history of philosophy.

Do you think you'll do anything like *The Mechanical Mind* again, for a wider audience?
I'd like to. So much good philosophy takes place in journals and is then read by very few people. If you write books, you want them to be read as widely as possible and have an impact.

Select Bibliography

The History of the Mind-Body Problem (edited with S. Patterson), Routledge, 2000

The Mechanical Mind: A Philosophical Introduction to Minds, Machines and Mental Representation, Penguin, 1995

'The mental causation debate', in *Proceedings of the Aristotelian Society, Supplementary Volume 69*, 1995

The Contents of Experience (editor), Cambridge University Press, 1992

'There is no question of physicalism', with D. H. Mellor, *Mind*, 99, 1990; reprinted in *Contemporary Materialism: A Reader*, edited by P. Moser and J. D. Trout, Routledge, 1995

8 The Concerns of Analytic Philosophy
In conversation with Michael Martin

There is a certain caricature of the type of British philosopher who came to be pre-eminent in the subject during the last century. Their style of philosophising is said to be 'analytic'. There are many for whom this epithet implies no value judgement, but for critics, it captures all that is dry and stale in the subject. The analytic philosopher models their thinking on mathematics and science. Unable to see in shades of grey, their cool logic always demands that a proposition is true or false. They will dissect any given concept with nit-picking precision, not because it is illuminating to do so, but for its own sake. The minutiae of their arguments become their overriding concern and they completely lose sight of why anyone would do philosophy in the first place. Berkeley remarked that philosophers had raised a dust and then complained they could not see. Analytic philosophers stand accused of attending so much to the particles that they can't even see the cloud.

A typical area of concern for such a philosopher is perception. Their starting point is a question of no small interest: what is our perceptual relationship to the real world? Is there a world that exists independently of ourselves, or does the world simply comprise our perceptions? To give a concrete example, when I see an apple, am I seeing something which exists, whether I see it or not; or is an apple no more than an assemblage of perceptions: colours, tastes and feels?

The question is a fascinating one, and one which often draws people into philosophising. However, our caricatured analytic philosopher bleeds the interest out of the question by a thousand fine distinctions. The most basic of these is between the perceiver, the perception and what the perception is of. For example, when I perceive an apple, there might be three different kinds of things in play: myself, the perceiver; the perceptions, of colour, taste and touch; and the apple, the thing itself. The problem now arises, if the perceiver is only directly aware of the perceptions, how does she gain knowledge of the thing itself? Indeed, how does she know there is a thing itself? Could the world contain nothing more than perceivers and perceptions? How would we ever know if it contained more, since on the model described we are denied perceptual access to things themselves?

These issues merely scratch the surface of the debate on perception that has run through analytic philosophy and which goes back at least as far as Locke in the seventeenth century. If the debate sounds interesting and invigorating, rather than tired and stale, you may well question the caricature of the analytic philosopher presented. After having read the details of the debate in more detail, where distinctions do become finer, you may persist with this impression or concur with the caricature after all. Perhaps there is no more to be said about this than that some people enjoy a style of argumentation which is close, tight and beholden of careful distinctions, whereas others prefer to paint with a broader brush. One philosopher's trawl through tedious minutiae is another one's exquisitely detailed intellectual landscape.

M. G. F. Martin is the real-world counterpart of our caricature. He works in the analytic tradition, is editor of perhaps its most distinguished journal, *Mind*, and his latest work is on the philosophy of perception. The issues sketched out above do form the background to his much more developed and detailed original work in the field. But, as is often the case, the reality is much richer than the caricature. Whether or not one warms to the kind of arguments that Martin deals with, to characterise his approach to the subject in the manner set out in the caricature would be a cruel distortion. What Martin has to say about philosophy may surprise those who have bought into the myth of analytic philosophy as a narrow discipline, in awe of science and logic. Acolytes may well commit the intellectual crimes the caricature represents, but the real McCoy knows better.

How did you come to focus on the philosophy of perception?

There are at least three different answers to that. One is just an anecdote, which is remembering writing my first essay on the causal theory of perception, which I found really puzzling and frustrating. The second involves taking the third person observation of my history: you might note that I was taught both as an undergraduate and supervised as a graduate by Paul Snowdon. He is one of the significant figures working on the philosophy of perception and was indeed working on it and doing interesting stuff when it was a very unfashionable topic. So you might notice a certain influence. And the third is that perception is just an interesting node for combining interests which overlap. There are issues in the philosophy of mind – thinking about the nature of consciousness and aspects of the human mind – and problems in epistemology, such as our access to the world. There are also issues in the philosophy of psychology: how we understand the link between the current science of the mind – such as how our visual system works, for instance – and how we naively think about the mind, which just seems very different. Perception has been such a perennial problem throughout western philosophy, but also one which reflects in quite interesting and slightly different ways, the different preoccupations in the shifts of the sciences, period to period. You get different pictures of perception depending on different scientific conceptions both of the world and how the mind interacts with the world.

The Anglophone tradition within which you work is often character-ised as being fairly ahistorical in its outlook. You've hinted that it is interesting to consider how the history of philosophy is related to the history of science. Do you think the tradition is not as ahistorical as it is sometimes presented, or do you have more of an interest in the history than perhaps some of your contemporaries?

Both are true. It's plainly the case that there are plenty of philosophers around who have no interest in history, as well as it always being the case that there are plenty who have. The clearest way in which the Anglophone tradition hasn't been historical in its methods is that it hasn't been the case that the mode of training is one through learning the history of philosophy above all else, and learning to comment on it. That remains the case. It is true of my upbringing, and the way I teach students. But there have always been important strands within the dis-cipline where people have been interested in the history of the subject and its relation to intellectual history.

But the way in which people discuss and analyse arguments in Anglophone philosophy doesn't tend to include a focus on the social or historical context which they came out of. There's none of that kind of social or historical deconstruction.

Well, when you've got an argument and it works, and you've clearly identified that the conclusion seems to follow from the premises, then there is no particular role for the historical context to come into play, possibly other than to explain why that argument became salient.

Issues of history come in because philosophers are notoriously inexplicit in their arguments. They'll give you enthymematic arguments, where premises are suppressed, so the question is, what further assumptions are in play? Why does this move seem pressing as opposed to that move? And you might think that even where you have perennial problems, such as I think the problems of perception are, that you need to look at what other assumptions are in play to understand why the problem gets formulated this way rather than that way. It's not deconstructing philosophy at all, or being sceptical about reason. It's just trying to understand the role of reason in relation to the different ways in which the world can seem problematic.

I've used the term the 'Anglophone tradition'. Is this synonymous with what has broadly been called the analytic tradition? Do you see yourself as working within the Anglophone tradition, the analytic tradition or both?

I don't mind either term. I'm not clear that there's a unique Anglophone tradition. Nor do I self-identify particularly with the label of the analytic tradition. There are clearly dominant strands within British universities – though less so Irish ones – and, for the large part, the major American universities, which are in common and reflect how philosophy departments were organised and developed in the twentieth century. I'm clearly part of that tradition.

If we use the analytic tradition as a broad term for that, what do you think are its main characteristics? What marks it out as a distinct mode of philosophy?

I'm not sure it is a distinct mode of philosophy. The key thing is to think that it's a form of academic philosophy. I think people don't necessarily maintain an adequate distinction between philosophy and academic philosophy. Academic philosophers have an interest in key texts, the canon of philosophy, which shifts and changes over time. There are certain key figures who, probably, almost everyone within the western tradition would agree belong in there. Those key texts tend to be of interest well beyond academic philosophical circles. On the whole, those texts were produced by non-academic philosophers. Some people decry that and think it's a terrible thing. But it's not clear that the point of academic philosophy is that it should itself produce such texts. It's nice if it does, but if it doesn't, it's not worthless. Academic philosophy tends to prosper partly as a matter of handing down certain traditions and skills of thought, problem seeking as well as problem solving, from generation to generation. It's in terms of that idea of a tradition in which people are trained that you can understand the analytic tradition and contrast it with, for instance, the current state of German philosophy. I think it's mistaken to think that there's a deep distinction in either doctrine or method in the published work produced in the two different traditions.

One feature of Anglophone academic philosophy is to do with the drawing out of what any particular position logically entails and its relation to other positions and propositions. I think part of that is the bringing out of assumptions, showing what is entailed at a foundational level, in order to hold any particular position.

I'm not sure that there's such an obsession with entailment and logical consequences. It may be part of the ideology of what people do, but notice that very few philosophers – certainly almost none of the ones who are interesting to read – give you explicitly valid arguments. There are certain styles of doing things where you do try to boil things down to the simplest set of so many premises and a conclusion, or an inconsistent set of assumptions, one of which you have to reject. But for that to be illuminating, you've got to get the right assumptions, ones which seem intuitively appealing, or correctly represent how we take the world to be in some aspect, and that is where the real work goes and that's where it gets hard. I really don't think that analytic philosophy is different from any other tradition of philosophy in trying to get a grip on what is intuitively fundamental.

You know from your own training, that part of what that training enables you to do is to tell a good piece of philosophy from a bad piece of philosophy. I can't describe for you a Turing machine which enables you to sort the good pieces of philosophy from the bad ones.

That's interesting, because the caricature of the Anglophone philosopher is the person who is obsessed with logic and aspires to a kind of quasi-scientific systematicity in argument. What you seem to be saying is that this is false, because at root what you're relying on is a kind of insight, where you can't specify what makes something a good piece of philosophy, it's just something that through training, skill and experience you come to recognise. That's much more touchy-feely than the stereotypical view of philosophy as it is done in British universities.

Yes, but very few people in British university philosophy departments have a training in logic and there's a kind of antipathy in British philosophy to doing things formally. In a way, I'm downplaying too much the importance of being able to formalise and systematise. It's very important to see what follows from the claims you make, to see what would lead you into a contradiction, and I think argument is very important. I like arguments, I like seeing where something goes right and wrong, and I tend to think they are an important part of philosophy. They're good philosophical tools to have, and it's clear that people's power of argument varies greatly. But it really would be a mistake to say that's what defines or what is distinctive about the analytic tradition.

Just putting forward a valid argument, even a sound argument, isn't necessarily going to succeed in getting someone to see things your way, because if they don't accept the conclusion, pointing out that the conclusion follows from the premises just directs them towards the question of which premise they should reject, or, even more obscurely, towards the possibility, given the way the premises are formulated, that some inexplicit assumption is being made which is illegitimate. Of course, having to do that can be very stimulating and challenging, and it can reframe philosophical problems. But you'd be missing the point if you thought it had all finished with writing down the argument.

I want to focus on some of your work and perhaps we can see how real philosophy operates by doing that. You discuss the distinction between sense datum theories and intentional theories, and see them as two responses to the same historical problem in the philosophy of perception. To start with, what is that problem?

The common problem is one you don't get to see just by looking at the most advantageous case of perception, for example, where you just see the apple and you see it as it is. That is to say, not only do you see the apple, but you see it's ripe, it's a certain shape, a certain variegated colour, and so on – and by seeing it you're in a position to see that it is so. It's a position that we hope we're in normally.

But there are problem cases in perception. One I particularly focus on is what philosophers tend to call hallucination. What philosophers mean by total hallucination is a situation where there is nothing in your ordinary, common, physical environment that you are aware of, but as far as you're concerned, you can't tell that. For example, you seem to see an apple, there's no way of telling your situation from one in which you're really seeing the apple, yet there's no physical apple there that you're seeing.

Now the thought is that we want some kind of account of what's going on with you when you're hallucinating. Moreover, many philosophers have been convinced that whatever's going on with you when you're perceiving, the very same kind of event must be occurring when you're having a perfectly matching hallucination – that is, a case where you really couldn't tell from the inside that it wasn't a perception of an apple.

Why do they think that?

There are at least two general kinds of grounds that people use for this. One is to say, if the subject can't tell any difference between these two situations, then that must mean subjectively, as a matter of what state the subject is undergoing, the two things are the same: the same kind of event is occurring in the two cases.

The other kind of reason they have is often what is called the causal argument in perception, and that's just to observe that given our general knowledge about how the world is structured, and also how our physiology is structured, we know that whatever kind of local, neurological causes are responsible for your seeing the apple, surely it's at least theoretically possible that the very same pattern of activity could have been produced in the absence of the apple. But if that pattern of activity is sufficient to bring about whatever mental state is in the one case your seeing the apple, then the same kind of activity could have brought about what in fact, given the absence of the apple, would have been a perfect hallucination of an apple. So, if you've got the same causal conditions producing an effect, then you must have the same kind of effect. So again, you must have the same kind of event in the case of perception and hallucination.

So if you accept this idea that you must have the same kind of psychological state when you're hallucinating as when you're perceiving, then any account of what's going on when you're perceiving must take into account that the same kind of thing can happen when you're hallucinating.

What we've got there is what seems like a perfectly reasonable assumption, but one that causes problems, because it proves to be incompatible with other basic assumptions we make about perception. What are those assumptions?

When you describe the perceptual situation from the subject's point of view, it looks like you want to say two things. First, in the case of the apple, that the situation involves the apple. In virtue of being situated as you are, when the apple's on the table in front of you, you are in a position to attend to the apple and make judgements about it, form desires involving it, and so on. The apple seems to be an aspect of your mental life. So that's the first thought, that the very objects of perception that we can interact with, that we can come to know about through our perception, are themselves aspects of our sensory experience of the world.

The second thought is that one of the key contrasts between sensing the world around us and merely thinking about the world or imagining aspects of the world in their absence, is that when you're perceiving something it really has to be there. It's a constituent of your experiential situation.

So our starting point, I would suggest, is what we might call a naive view of perception which says that in the perceptual situation, when things are as advantageous as they could be – the apple's there and you're seeing it the way it is – the apple and various of its features are part of the experiential event.

Why does that naive view run into problems when you combine it with the view that the very same kind of event can occur when you're hallucinating as when you're perceiving?

When you're hallucinating there doesn't have to be an apple there at all. We could have destroyed all of the apples in the world, but still if we'd managed to get the causal situation right, we could have produced an experience just like the one of having the apple. So, in the case of such a hallucination, we have two choices. One is that an apple doesn't have to exist for you to have an experience in this way, so a hallucination is much more like a case of imagination or thinking, in that it can involve an object without its existence. The other is that hallucination does have to involve the existence of some object, but as there is no mind-independent object perceived in hallucination – no actual apple is there – what is perceived would have to be a mind-dependent object, what is usually called a sense datum. But now, if the kind of experience you're having when hallucinating merely involves a sense datum, so having the experience of a sense datum is sufficient to bring about the experience of the object, then having such an experience is sufficient to bring about the object of awareness even if you *were* perceiving.

So either way it looks like, if the account of the perceptual experience also needs to be an account of hallucinatory experience, then either we have to give up the idea that the object perceived literally has to be a constituent of the experience; or if there has to be an object there, then the kind of object that would have to be there would have to be a mind-dependent one, a sense datum.

How do the sense datum and intentional approaches map onto these alternatives?

What's distinctive of the sense datum approach is that it holds onto the idea that there's a contrast between sensing and imagining or thinking, and says what's distinctive about sensing is that something actually has to be there if I'm having a sense experience. So it bites the bullet in relation to hallucination, and says that what I'm aware of is something which is guaranteed to be there just by bringing about an experience and so it will be mind dependent.

What is distinctive about the intentional approach is that it holds on to the other desideratum, that surely our experience relates us to or is an awareness of a mind-independent world. What that means is that in the case of hallucination, there just isn't anything that we're aware of, nothing that really exists. So the kind of experience we have is the kind of event which doesn't require the existence of an object, so in that sense it's more like thought and imagination.

You don't find either alternative appealing. Why not?

A problem with making either move is that if the reason we think we have to try and reconcile these three assumptions is precisely that when we're trying to give an adequate account of what our experience is like, we're inclined both to affirm that the subject matter of experience is mind-independent *and* that what is distinctive of experience is that it actually has as a constituent what its subject matter is, what it is directed upon. Giving up either of these principles would lead us to the conclusion that experience is other than it seems to be. So you end up having some form of error theory of perception, which says our experience is not as it seems to us to be, as bizarre as that might be.

So now the thought is that if you're forced to embrace an error theory of perception, what you're saying is that in general our experience really is not as it seems to us to be. If that's the case, then really introspection on our experience, reflection on what our experience is like is not a good guide to the nature of experience, because we're massively in error, according to either of these two approaches. If that's so, then the initial, intuitive thought that really hallucination and perception must be the same kind of event because what you're trying to capture is what things are like for a subject, has been undermined. The whole point of either approach is to say that how things are to the subject, in the sense of how you would reflect on what your experience is like, is really not how experience can be anyway.

So maybe we should more conservatively suggest that actually the assumption that the same kind of thing must be going on when you're perceiving as when you're hallucinating is wrong. The fact that a subject won't necessarily notice the difference between them doesn't establish that the very same thing is going on. So instead we might say, it's true when you're perceiving that the objects independent of the mind are constituents of your experience, so to be experiencing like this they literally have to be there; yet it's not the case that the same kind of event is occurring when you're hallucinating, so the same conditions don't hold of it. Rather, what's distinctive in general of hallucinating is just it's the kind of situation in which you can't tell just by reflection that you're not in one of the perceptual states. This has come to be known as the disjunctive approach to perception, the view that perceptual and hallucinatory experiences are different.

Your argument reminds me of the passage from Russell, in which he says naive realism leads to physical science which, if true, undermines naive realism. What you're saying is that you start with an intuitive reflection on what perception is like, and the belief that there is something the same going on in hallucination and perception, and that motivates both the sense datum and the intentional theories. Both theories conclude by saying we are fundamentally mistaken about how we understand perception, but that under-mines the grounds which motivated the theories themselves.

Exactly. That's precisely what I'm trying to do.

From what you've said, it seems that temperamentally you're on the side of common sense to a certain extent, in that there's some-thing important which needs to be preserved in our common-sense understanding of our own mental lives.

I think that's right, and I think that's just an aspect of where the philosophical impulse starts from. You've got to try to get self-understanding, and part of your self-understanding is reflecting on how things are for you now, as they are around you. So your common-sense understanding of how things are for you now is in one sense bedrock. Even if it's in some way going to turn out to be an illusion, and in a deep sense things aren't really as they seem to you, that may seem to you a part of the bedrock which needs as accurate a description as you can achieve, as well as some explanation of how things can be so.

You would agree that there are many issues, arguments and methods which cut across the Anglophone/continental divide in the philosophy of perception. But why then, if you look at the Anglophone literature and your own footnotes, are there so few references to continental philosophers and so many to peers in the British and American schools?

If you're asking a biographical question I guess the answer is just that I happen to have studied early British figures writing on perception in more detail. That's to say I know in reasonable detail, Moore, Russell, Broad and Price, and earlier figures like Prichard and Cook-Wilson. Although I have some knowledge of Husserl, Sartre, Merleau-Ponty and a bit of Brentano, I don't have any serious knowledge of them. It takes half a lifetime to have serious knowledge of those figures. So my references to them are more cautious. Actually, if you look at the people cited in my footnotes, you'll find that most of them have been more recent figures and there aren't recent phenomenologists. There are recent writers in German and French traditions, so why haven't I referenced them? Well, there you can go back to the sociological points we were talking about before where, so to speak, academic conversations can pull apart and you have an audience with whom you have certain common assumptions.

Is that something you should be phlegmatic about? Is it worrying that for sociological reasons, the frames of reference of philosophers are set by local sociological reasons rather than consideration of who or what might be the best writers to shed light on the puzzle? The concern is that people just aren't reading those who might be perennial figures.

I guess if that's true then that would be a problem. I don't see any particular reason not to be phlegmatic because I don't think there's a general answer about whom you should be reading. On the whole, you ought to be reading as broadly as you can, but also in as much depth as you can and there's a limited amount of time that you can study. On the whole, I think philosophers are better if they have some knowledge of the history of their subject, so you ought not to be extremely narrow, but there are good examples of brilliant philosophers who paint with a very small palate of figures with whom they engage. So general prescriptions here are, I think, foolish.

You've just completed a substantial book on perception. Do you know where you're going to go from here in your future work?

I have various projects that I've been working on already which will take some time to complete. One longer term project that I do have an interest in is the idea that one of the things that is distinctive about the mind as a subject area that we study, is the idea that you shouldn't over-theorise about it, that there's a way in which aspects of the mind are all on the surface. Whereas it's fine within psychology proper to posit all kinds of hidden springs of action, thought and so on, you've got to be very careful about importing that into the common-sense picture of the mind, and failing to see that there's a division between the two things and a problem about how the one fits on top of the other.

Select Bibliography

Uncovering Appearances, Oxford University Press, 2002

The History of the Problems of Perception (edited with M. Stone), Routledge, 2001

'Out of the past: episodic recall as retained acquaintance,' in *Time and Memory*, edited by C. Hoerl and T. McCormack, Clarendon Press, 2001

'Beyond dispute: sense-data, intentionality and the mind-body problem', in *History of the Mind-Body Problem*, edited by T. Crane and S. Patterson, Routledge, 2000

'An eye directed outward,' in *Knowing Our Own Minds*, edited by C. Wright, B. Smith and C. Macdonald, Clarendon Press, 1998

9 On Vagueness

In conversation with Timothy Williamson

If one considers how a term like 'tall' is ordinarily employed in the English language then it is clear that its meaning is ambiguous. Quite simply, its meaning varies relative to the context in which it is employed. For example, compared to other buildings in the United Kingdom, the Canada Tower at Canary Wharf, in London, is tall. But if you ask whether it is tall compared to the Empire State Building in Manhattan, you will get the answer that it is not.

Ambiguity does not appear to be an intractable philosophical problem. It seems that one can eliminate ambiguity by qualifying a term, and thereby fixing its meaning. For example, as above, rather than asking whether a building is tall, you can ask whether it is tall compared to some other building; or, to give a different example, rather than asking whether it is hot in the south of France during the summer, you can ask whether it is hot compared to the usual summer weather in the United Kingdom.

However, consider the following question: if the average height of a man in the United Kingdom is 1.75 metres, what is the minimum height of a tall man in the United Kingdom? It seems impossible to answer this question for a reason that is not to do with ambiguity. Rather, it seems that the problem has to do with the fact that there will always be borderline cases where it is not clear that the term tall applies. Is a 1.8 metres man tall? The correct answer seems to be – 'well, maybe'.

One thought might be that it is possible to decide such a question simply by specifying that any male of 1.8 metres height and above is tall. However, this is just to avoid the problem by means of definitional fiat. The word 'tall', as it is normally employed, does not seem to have this kind of precision; it appears to be a *vague* concept. It should be clear that this is not a problem of ambiguity. It is not that the word tall has different meanings in different contexts. Rather, as indicated above, the problem is that certain concepts just appear to be *vague* with respect to borderline cases.

The philosophical problem of vagueness is tied up with what is known as the Sorites paradox. Consider the following scenario:

> You're asked whether 1,000 stones make a heap. You reply that together they do make a heap. You're then asked whether taking one stone away from a heap can make the difference between it being heap and not a heap. You reply that it cannot make such a difference. So it must be that 999 stones are a heap. What about 998 stones? Yes, that's a heap too! And 997 stones . . . ? You then realise that you have a problem. What happens if, one by one, stones are removed until you have only one stone left? It seems that you are required to claim that one stone makes a heap. You've already insisted that taking any one stone from a heap cannot make it a non-heap. However, one stone doesn't make a heap, so something has gone wrong with the argument. The problem is that it isn't clear what.

This is the Sorites paradox. It seems that the reasoning is correct. It *doesn't* seem possible that taking one stone away from any number of stones can make the difference between 'heap' and 'not-heap'. In other words, 'heap' seems to be a vague concept that does not have a sharp cut-off point. But it is also clear that the conclusion that follows if one accepts this premise is false. So we're left with a contradiction between the facts as we know them (that 1,000 stones do make a heap, but one stone doesn't) and the conclusion of the argument.

What is the way out of this paradox? According to Timothy Williamson, it is necessary to deny the premise that taking one stone away from a heap can never make it a non-heap. In other words, it is necessary to argue that vague terms do in fact have sharp boundaries. In this instance, it amounts to the claim that there is a number of stones for which subtracting one stone makes the difference between there being a heap and there not being a heap. For many philosophers, this is a highly counter-intuitive notion, for it seems to require what Roy Sorensen calls a 'linguistic miracle'. However, it is for this position that Williamson argues at length in his 1994 book *Vagueness*.

I believe that you have been interested in philosophy since you were very young?

Yes, I was exposed to philosophy at a very early age. My great uncle, Nathan Isaacs, who was one of the people who helped to introduce the works of Piaget into Great Britain, read papers on philosophy to the Aristotelian Society. And he was somebody whom I talked to when I was a very young child, so I had some sort of early sense of philosophy as an enjoyable form of abstract argument. In my teens, I started reading bits and pieces, I did a little bit of logic, and I studied mathematics at school. When I heard that it was possible to do a degree in mathematics and philosophy, it just seemed obvious that that was what would suit me temperamentally. As soon as I started learning formal logic, that struck me as exactly the language that I wanted to think in.

Were your early philosophical interests purely in the abstractions of logic, or did you have other interests?

There were other interests. I was interested in free will. Even very early, I was interested in issues about the idea of approximate truth. Any topic that was susceptible to abstract argument of a philosophical style was something that I was prepared to talk about.

At what point did you come to concentrate on logic?

I suppose as soon as I started working for my first degree, I found logic something that I could do without too much difficulty, and it struck me as something deeply satisfying. So certainly as a first-year undergraduate, I already thought of logic as what I wanted to make my career in.

It's interesting that you made this decision so early on. This special-isation places you firmly within the tradition of Anglo-American philosophy. I wonder how you view other kinds of philosophy – for example, what one might call continental philosophy?

Of course, many kinds of philosophy are grouped under that label. From the standpoint of a place like Oxford, which is a centre of analytic philosophy, and where one feels comfortable in pursuing that form of philosophy, and where it is not at all under threat, it is easy to make conciliatory remarks about continental philosophy. The people that I know who are most hostile to continental philosophy are analytic philosophers who have been most exposed to it, in particular those working in continental Europe, for example in France and Italy, who until recently found it extremely hard to get jobs because of the dominance of continental schools in their universities.

I don't want to give the impression that I think nothing of value is done under the aegis of continental philosophy. That would be far too crude a view. But certain advances in philosophical standards have been made within analytic philosophy, and for anyone who has taken these to heart, there would be a serious loss of integrity involved in abandoning them in the way that would be required to participate in continental philosophy as currently practised.

Out of your early interest in logic, you developed an interest in vagueness and indeterminable truth. How did this emerge?

My doctoral thesis was on the idea of approximation to the truth, which is really an idea associated with Karl Popper. The idea is that we can preserve the notion that science aims at some sort of objective truth, in spite of the way that scientific theories are constantly being revised and found to be incorrect, by thinking of them as successive approximations to the truth. This means that even if science never gets to the truth, it gets closer and closer. That's not a problem strictly speaking about vagueness, because all these theories in principle might be completely precise, but looking back I can see that there was some subterranean connection in my mind between these concerns and my later concerns.

And if we trace it even further back, as a first year undergraduate, I was interested in the non-transitivity of indiscriminability. So, for example, if one takes a spectrum of colours from yellow to red, it might be that given a series of colour samples along that spectrum, each sample is indiscriminable by the naked eye from the next one, even though the samples at either end of the series are blatantly different from each other.

I was interested in the question of how one could define a notion of identity of perceived colour for a series like that, when, on the one hand, each sample is the same perceived colour as the next, and at the same time at the extremes there are different perceived colours. I proved a little formal result, showing that although one couldn't have exactly the intuitive idea of a perceived colour because it is incoherent in this way, one could in a precise sense have a best approximation to it. And that kind of problem is in fact very intimately connected with the Sorites paradox, which is the way in which vagueness became a problem in philosophy.

Following on from this, could you detail in broad terms the problem of vagueness, with reference to the Sorites paradox?
A simple way of grasping the Sorites paradox is by doing a thought experiment. Imagine a heap of sand. Imagine one grain subtracted from the heap and ask yourself whether what remains is still a heap. And the natural answer to give is that it is, because it seems that one grain is far too small for it to make a difference. But in that case what the thought experiment seems to support is the principle that the result of subtracting one grain from a heap is still a heap. The problem is that if one applies that principle over and over again, one gets the result that there is a heap when there are only three grains left, only two grains, one grain and none.

So one's second thought is that it seems to follow that there must have been a grain such that one had a heap and one took that grain away and then there was no longer a heap. But that is found very implausible by many people, because they think that the concept of a heap is too vague and casual to allow for that kind of very sharp cut-off between heaps and non-heaps.

The trouble is that it seems to be really quite simple logic that drives us into saying that there *is* such a cut-off. Consequently, many people have thought that standard forms of reasoning don't work for vague concepts. In particular, classical logic, as it is standardly used, is based on the idea that there is a dichotomy of all statements into the true and the false – every statement is either true or false, and no statement is both. Some people have thought that that dichotomy doesn't apply to vague statements, one needs something like a continuum of degrees of truth, and that in turn has all sorts of implications for what reasoning is valid for vague concepts.

The problem of vagueness, then, is the problem of what logic is correct for vague concepts, and correspondingly what notions of truth and falsity are applicable to vague statements.

In your book *Vagueness*, you suggest that the Sorites paradox has been particularly problematic for the Stoics and for analytic philosophy. Presumably, certainly with analytic philosophers, the problem has to do with the precision of logical language.

I think that it's a problem that you're unlikely to worry about very much if you're not very serious about logic, because it is a problem about the exact form of valid reasoning. The Stoics were the leading logicians of antiquity, in their own time they were more important logicians than Aristotle, so they were worried about it. After them, logic went through a bad period, and most of the works of the Stoics were lost. Then with the revival of logic in the twentieth century, where philosophers following Frege and Russell have been concerned to give exact statements of the principles of valid reasoning, the Sorites paradox has had to be confronted, because of the standards that are being set. One attitude has been that the sort of logic that they were defining was applicable only to absolutely precise language, for mathematics and possibly the most abstract sort of science. But since just about all the concepts that we ordinarily use, not just in everyday life, but in empirical science, are vague, that leaves a huge vacuum for what the appropriate standards of reasoning are.

What kind of attempts have been made to solve this problem?

By far the best known attempt outside philosophy is what is known as 'fuzzy logic', which is based on the notion of a continuum of degrees of truth. It has a well-chosen name, and good public relations, but it is based on, in my view, a badly flawed technical framework, so the kind of consequence that it has is the following.

Suppose that we have identical twins, let's say that they are physically alike in every way, and let's suppose that they are both borderline cases for the concept 'tall'. Let's say that it is half true of one twin that he's tall, which is the kind of judgement that fuzzy logic allows one to make. Then, of course, it will equally be half true of the other twin that he's tall, because he's the same height. And one can show that fuzzy logic is committed to the judgement that it is also half true that one twin is tall and the other is not. But what seems to be clearly the case here is that it is completely false that one twin is tall and the other is not, because they are the same height. And that sort of commitment is a consequence of the formal structure of fuzzy logic.

There are other approaches to vagueness that challenge the classical assumption of bivalence – the idea that every statement is either true or false, and not both – that are technically more sophisticated than fuzzy logic. But what I've argued in *Vagueness* is that none of these alternative logics or treatments of truth and falsity really gives a satisfactory account of the problem, all of them can be shown to have technical flaws that mean that they have to be rejected.

It seems that the worry about vagueness has to do with the requirement that statements about the world should be bivalent. But perhaps it might be claimed that such statements are not actually about the world in the kind of way that we suppose, they just don't function in a way that requires them to be bivalent. Suppose I make the statement that a person is thin. Could this statement be a kind of intuition device, which is supposed to signal something to the person who hears it, but which makes no claim to bivalence?

Well, you certainly mean something to which the ideas of truth and falsity are applicable. I once met a philosopher whom previously I'd known only from his published works. For some reason I had formed a preconception that he was thin, and I met him and realised that I had been wrong, and I tactlessly told him so! In that instance, my previous belief that he was thin turned out to be false. There was a simple disagreement between my later belief that he was not thin, and my earlier belief that he was thin. It was precisely my later realisation that he was not thin that forced me to reject my belief that he was thin, so that rejection of my earlier mistake depended on the incompatibility of the statement that he is not thin with the statement that he is thin. It's hard to see how one could learn from experience without that kind of incompatibility.

Might someone reply that, in the situation that you describe, you might be mistaken about the kind of statement that you are making when you say that someone is thin? Therefore, you may well think that your previous statement is falsified by your experience, but in fact you're just making a mistake about the kind of statement you were originally making. And, of course, we do make mistakes about the kind of statements that we make.

It's certainly a possibility that one could be confused about what one was doing in uttering certain words. But the thing to remember is that just about everything we say is vague to some extent. It follows that if the vagueness of a statement meant that it wasn't really a statement about the world, then we will never succeed in making statements about the world, except possibly in mathematics. And if that means that the ideas of truth and falsity simply don't apply, then that would mean that we will just about never be mistaken, when it seems to me that one of the most central facts about our lives is that we are often mistaken.

In *Vagueness*, and in contrast to most philosophers, you advocate an epistemic view of vagueness. Can you explain what's involved in this view, and also why most philosophers find it so counter-intuitive?

The central idea is extremely simple, it is just that in every case it is either true or false to apply whatever vague concept is in question, and not both. But in borderline cases what is going on is that it is impossible to know which of the two truth values, truth or falsity, one's statement has, so the epistemic view is that vagueness is a certain kind of inescapable ignorance.

Much of the original opposition to that view came from the assumption that it would be impossible to explain the source of the ignorance. In fact, I myself was an opponent of the epistemic view, until I began to see how the ignorance might be explained. The rough idea is that in order to avoid ignorance, to attain knowledge, one has to make judgements that are true with a certain reliability, and that if one is very close to a conceptual boundary, then one's judgement will be too unreliable to constitute knowledge, and therefore one will be ignorant.

I argued in the book that those kinds of limitations on knowledge can be found in all sorts of spheres – for example, in perception – and what's distinctive about vagueness is simply that the margins for error have a conceptual rather than perceptual source, they have to do with our inability fully to appreciate the nature of our own concepts.

Can you briefly say what it is that fixes the meaning of our concepts, so that there is a matter of fact about their truth or falsity?

I have the same view, in a way, as most philosophers about what fixes the reference of a term like, for example, 'thin'. It depends on the way in which ordinary speakers use the term, it depends also on the particular conversational context in which they are using it, and it depends on the way in which that use is causally connected with the environment in which they are speaking and acting.

I think where many philosophers have gone wrong is in expecting a kind of transparency in the relation between the factors that determine reference and their outcome, the reference itself, so that, to put it crudely, one should be able to calculate the reference on the basis of those factors. On my view, we can't expect to find any precise formula that would enable one to make such a calculation. So although we can be acquainted with the factors that fix a reference, that doesn't put us in a position to say exactly what reference is fixed.

So your view is that if I say Timothy Williamson is 'thin', then the reference is fixed through usage and various other things, so that there is a matter of fact about that statement?

Yes. That's right.

Can we explore this a bit further? Suppose I live on the east coast of America, and I use the word 'thin'. You'd presumably accept that it might have a very different meaning in this context, than it would if I were living in one of the southern states of America?

That's true, but it's not inconsistent with my view, because there's a very general phenomenon of context dependence in language, that what an expression refers to very often depends on the context in which it is used. The simplest example of this is a word such as 'I', which refers to the speaker, so the reference varies according to who is speaking, and that case shows that this kind of contextual variation doesn't need to have anything particularly to do with vagueness.

I wonder if a critic might respond that there is a worry that vagueness will enter into contextual dependence. Suppose, for example, I've been brought up in one of the southern states of America, but I'm now living on the east coast, and I'm talking to an audience made up of two sets of people, half from the southern states of America, half from New York. What fixes the meaning of the word 'thin' in that kind of context – where you're talking to different audiences of different backgrounds, and where your own background is not straightforward?

Well it's true that vagueness and context dependence interact in very complicated ways, and so what one has to do as a theoretician is to tease out those two different influences, but the key thing to remember is that the claim of bivalence is simply that when one makes a statement, the statement is either true or false. Now the statement that one makes may depend not just on the words that one uses, but on the context in which one uses them.

You've described an extremely complex context, where there is perhaps some tension between the speaker's background and the hearers' background, and that kind of complexity is one that can arise in principle, irrespective of vagueness. So, for example, let's take the expression 'the first floor', which in some places refers to the ground floor, and in other places refers to the floor above the ground floor. That's not a matter of vagueness. If somebody uses that expression in a context in which people differ in their expectations about that word, it may be hard to say what's correct. And that will in turn depend on the extent to which the speaker is deferring to the hearers' use, and the extent to which the hearers are deferring to the speaker's use, and there may be other very subtle social factors. But remember that I'm not attempting to give a formula for what the right answer will be. The context may be highly complex in ways which make it hard to say what the right answer is, but it seems a mistake to say that that is evidence that there is no right answer.

I'll ask one more question, because perhaps not everybody will yet be persuaded. The case you describe where the expression 'the first floor' can refer differently seems clear. But it is a lot more complicated where the person uttering the statement herself inhabits different contexts. For example, they might have had a radically schizophrenic upbringing in terms of their becoming familiar with the rules of particular languages. Consider this scenario: you have a person who in one context, hermetically sealed, and in which she has lived half her life, has learnt that thin refers to people who are under sixteen stone. And in the other context, again hermetically sealed, and in which she has lived the other half of her life, she has learnt that thin refers to people under ten stone. And let's say that she is talking to an audience comprising people who have shared neither of these upbringings. In this situation, it seems almost inconceivable that there is anything that can fix the precise meaning of the word 'thin'.

I think if one was actually going to investigate such a case, one would like to know something about the dispositions of speakers and hearers, one would like to know something about how the conversation might actually go, when they realise that there was this difference of expectations and standards between them. I think most philosophers of language, even those who oppose the epistemic view, would agree that at least in some cases the conversation would go in a way that would reveal that one standard was the correct one, in cases where there was a strong predisposition to agree on a certain standard, but opponents of epistemicism would hold that there might be some cases where if there is no agreement, there would be no right answer. The epistemicists would be more inclined to say that the very fact of disagreement would be one of the relevant factors that would determine the reference.

I think the kind of frustration that you may be feeling is character-istic of philosophers who oppose the epistemic view, and it is an extremely natural one, because where reference is determined, if one has any curiosity, one wants to understand how reference is determined.

An important point to recognise, though, is that it is part of the epistemic view not simply that we are in fact ignorant of these matters, but that we are inescapably ignorant in that we have no idea of any kind of investigation we could carry out that would answer these questions. In particular, we have no idea about how we could carry out an investi-gation that would lead to the discovery of a formula for calculating reference. That's a very disappointing result, because it suggests that there are limits to our understanding that we cannot surpass. But we may have to live with that.

Are there any more general lessons to be learned from the system-atic nature of our ignorance? I think you've argued that rational thinkers are not always in a position to know what the evidence is for any particular proposition.

One of the things that I've been doing since publishing *Vagueness* is looking at ways in which the argument of *Vagueness* can be generalised to issues about our knowledge that are not particularly connected to vagueness itself. In particular, I think those arguments can be used to show that all distinctions that we can make within the realm of our experience are problematic in some cases, and that means that the distinction between what is evidence for our other beliefs, and what is not evidence, is itself sometimes going to be a problematic one.

Philosophers have typically worked with the idea that there is some basic level at which we can sort out the evidence that we have for testing our theories from what is not evidence, so, as it were, if we reflect carefully enough on our experience we can see what evidential basis we have against which we can test our beliefs. So they've thought that there is a relatively unproblematic distinction between evidence and non-evidence, so long as one reflects carefully enough. And I think that that can be shown to be fallacious on the basis of these epistemological considerations.

How have philosophers responded to your advocacy of the epistemic view?
The first wave of response was along the lines that people could not believe the view, but they were surprised that so much could be said in its favour. It was found a frustrating view, in the sense that people wanted to argue against it, but they could see that epistemicists had replies to the arguments that they were producing, so that in effect they were forced into the position of saying that they just had a direct intuition that epistemicism is false. But obviously it's not clear that an intuition that a philosophical theory is false is terribly convincing.

My sense is that now it is to some extent a generational matter. I wouldn't want to say that the epistemic view is dominant among the young people in the area, but it is now attracting larger numbers of adherents, particularly amongst those entering the field for the first time. I don't expect it ever to become an uncontentious view, because one doesn't expect that in philosophy, but it's fairly clear that it has been accepted as one of the main views of vagueness that has to be considered.

Are you still working on these kinds of issues? Or are you moving on to new things now?

Well, I've just published a book on epistemology. After that, I want to work on a different sort of issue about an area known as modal metaphysics, about the nature of possible beings. To give an example of the kind of problem that I'm interested in, we can say that J. F. Kennedy and Marilyn Monroe could have had a child, and the issue arises of whether one can say that there is such a thing as a possible child of JFK and Marilyn Monroe. If so, what sort of thing is it? This is an area which is susceptible of quite rigorous logical analysis, but it is one that suggests that the nature of existence is very different from what people usually take it to be.

Select Bibliography

Knowledge and Its Limits, Clarendon Press, 2000

'Scepticism and evidence', *Philosophy and Phenomenological Research*, 60: 3, 2000

'The broadness of the mental: some logical considerations', in *Philosophical Perspectives 12: Language, Mind and Ontology*, edited by J. Tomberlin, Blackwell, 1998

'Cognitive homelessness', *The Journal of Philosophy*, 93: 11, 1996

Vagueness, Routledge, 1994

10   The Rebirth of Metaphysics

In conversation with **Robin Le Poidevin**

The nineteenth-century British judge, Charles Bowen, is said to have characterised a metaphysician as 'A blind man in a dark room – looking for a black hat, which isn't there'. More seriously, but in a similar vein, the philosopher, F. H. Bradley (1846–1924), in his book, *Appearance and Reality*, claimed that 'Metaphysics is the finding of bad reasons for what we believe upon instinct; but to find these reasons is no less an instinct'.

What is it about metaphysics that has led to these kinds of judgements? The answer to this question has partly to do with its subject matter. Broadly defined, metaphysics is the enquiry into the nature of ultimate reality. Under this rubric, philosophers since Aristotle have been concerned to analyse the nature of being, the existence of God, the nature of causality, the nature of time, and other similar issues.

Of course, what they say about these things varies. Taking the nature of being as an example, it is possible to distinguish, amongst others, between materialist and idealist philosophers. The doctrine of materialism asserts that all existent entities and processes are made up of matter or are an attribute or effect of matter. For example, a strict or 'eliminative' materialism will claim that mental phenomena (beliefs, desires and feelings, etc.) simply do not exist. The doctrine of idealism takes the opposite view. It asserts that mind is the most fundamental reality, and that the material world is either in some way dependent on mind or actually has a mental character itself.

With both of these doctrines, one gets a sense of how the enterprise of metaphysics might arouse the suspicion of certain people. Perhaps most significantly, these kinds of theories make claims that go beyond what can be justified on purely evidential grounds. For example, it is argued that the claim that nothing exists except material reality is one that can never be settled by an appeal to evidence. What then follows from this fact that metaphysics often seeks to go beyond what is evidentially given?

The first point to make is that in some ways this is not a criticism at all. A metaphysician can simply respond: 'Of course metaphysics seeks to look beyond the evidence, that's the whole point of metaphysics!' In this regard, it is significant that a lot of metaphysical analyses have been rooted in purely a priori reasoning (that is, reasoning which doesn't make any reference to experience). However, there are nevertheless worries associated with this approach.

The first is the fairly limited worry that without the necessity to ground metaphysical theories in the world of experience there will be a tendency for philosophers to engage in flights of fancy. This worry is often associated with a critical reaction to the great 'system building' philosophers – such as G. W. F. Hegel. The second, perhaps more serious, worry is that metaphysical claims are rendered meaningless by their lack of evidential grounding. This criticism is associated with philosophers such as A. J. Ayer. He claimed, along with other logical positivists, that meaningful statements have to be either true as a matter of logic or verifiable by experience. In terms of these criteria, it is fairly easy to show that many metaphysical statements are not meaningful.

How has metaphysics stood up to these criticisms? According to Robin Le Poidevin, the beginning of the twenty-first century finds metaphysics in pretty good health. It is true that the subject buckled for a while under the assault from logical positivism. However, the last three decades of the twentieth century saw a revival in its fortunes. Partly, this had to do with the decline in influence of logical positivism, but it is also because the nature of metaphysics has changed. The grand cosmic visions of the nineteenth century are largely a thing of the past. Twenty-first century metaphysics is a much more grounded discipline.

You've written on a number of the 'big questions', particularly, on the nature of time and the existence of God. Were these issues that interested you when you were growing up?

I think I took God for granted when I was growing up, at least until I was about fourteen. But I do remember being intrigued at the age of nine or ten by the question: Why was it that of all the people in the world just one of them happened to be me? And what did it mean for one person to be me?

Another problem that used to intrigue me was to do with time, and particularly the passage of time. I was very interested in the idea that the moment you try to think about or concentrate on the present, it has just receded into the past.

Given that you were thinking about these kinds of issues, did you progress quite naturally into philosophy?

I certainly didn't think at the age of nine or ten that this was a subject that you could study. The turning point came when I was sixteen, and I had already chosen my A levels, and had intended to go for a career in medicine. Then I came across *The Age of Reason*, by Jean-Paul Sartre, and I was absolutely fascinated by his account of this philosophy lecturer, and his desire to live a life that was completely unconstrained by external circumstances and other people. He strikes me as a rather less attractive character now, by the way: too selfish! I also read Sartre's *Nausea*, and then I started to become interested in questions of existence – what it was to exist and whether things had fundamental natures. Eventually, I decided that medicine was not for me, and that I would read philosophy at university.

Did you retain an interest in existentialism at university or did you quite quickly get taken up by the concerns of analytic philosophy?

I didn't study existentialism, and it would be true to say that I became almost exclusively interested in what is now known as analytic philosophy. One of the papers that I had to take for my university entrance exam was a paper in logic, which I much enjoyed. And one of the first things that I studied at university was Hume's *Enquiry Concerning Human Understanding*, and that, of course, raises a number of metaphysical issues.

So was it out of this that your interest in metaphysics developed?

At Oxford, where I studied for my first degree, I didn't actually take a paper in metaphysics. In fact, I don't think that was even an option. But nevertheless, metaphysical issues certainly cropped up in the papers that I did take. I remember looking at a past examination paper, and coming across the question: Why is there something rather than nothing? This absolutely fascinated me. I had no idea how to go about answering such a question, but it is a fundamental metaphysical issue.

I also remember being struck by a few particular arguments. For example, I read Derek Parfit's article on personal identity, where he asks how we would view the identity of persons over time, if we lived in a world where a person could split into two. This had a great influence on me. I was also excited by Kripke's suggestion that if we could think of a mental state occurring without an accompanying physical state, this showed that it was logically possible for the mental to exist without the physical, and therefore, since all identities are necessary, that the mental and physical are quite distinct.

I think what appealed to me about these arguments was the fact that you could think about the nature of the world through purely a priori considerations, without actually having recourse to experience or indeed science.

The whole project of metaphysics came under attack from certain quarters in the twentieth century. What was found objectionable about metaphysics?

I see three different kinds of attacks on metaphysics in the twentieth century. Perhaps the most obvious and dramatic was the challenge from logical positivism, whose most prominent exponent in this country was A. J. Ayer. The logical positivists advanced a criterion of meaningfulness for any statement that one might make about the world. Either it is a truth of logic or it is empirically verifiable. They felt that metaphysical statements simply failed this test of meaningfulness – that metaphysical statements weren't just logical truths, but neither could they be verified by experience. So they were rejected as meaningless.

Can you give an example of the kind of metaphysical statement that logical positivists had a problem with?

I'll give an example from Ayer's *Language, Truth and Logic*. I think he's chosen a rather easy target, and it gives you an idea of the kind of things that counted as metaphysics in the early part of the twentieth century. This is a remark taken from Bradley's *Appearance and Reality* – 'The Absolute enters into, but is itself incapable of, evolution and progress'. Ayer doesn't have any difficulty showing that this is not verifiable.

But, of course, there are less esoteric metaphysical propositions, such as, for example, that every event has a cause, which appear to be entirely intelligible, but which are neither definitional nor conclusively verifiable. Ayer recognises this, and he doesn't want to throw out every generalisation. Even in *Language, Truth and Logic*, he understands that it's no good demanding that a statement be conclusively verifiable; it is enough to be able to produce evidence in favour or against it.

Ayer ran into trouble with his whole thesis, in that his claim that statements about the world had either to be logical truths or empirically verifiable, was itself neither a logical truth nor empirically verifiable.

Absolutely. It has often been said on those grounds that logical positivism is self-defeating. This may partly account for its demise. One might attempt to get around it by saying that the principle of verification itself is a rule rather than a statement of fact. So we don't take it as true or false, but simply as something that guides us.

You mentioned that there were three attacks on metaphysics. What were the other two?

Later on in the century, around the 1950s, there arose a quite different form of attack from linguistic or ordinary language philosophy. And here perhaps the best known exponents would be Gilbert Ryle and J. L. Austin, both working in Oxford.

They looked at how one decides about the meaning of a particular statement. And they asserted that if one wants to know, for example, what the words 'cause', 'truth' or 'justice' mean, one shouldn't look for some extra linguistic reality to which they might attach. Rather, one simply looks at how they are used in ordinary discourse. They had no time for metaphysical speculation – the desire to get beyond the world of language and appearance to some kind of transcendent reality.

The final attack on metaphysics – and this is an idea which crops up repeatedly in the history of philosophy, though one form of it was particularly prominent in the last quarter of the twentieth century – is the suggestion that it isn't possible to give a description of the world which is from absolutely no point of view whatsoever. It could be said that it is a metaphysical ideal to do precisely this, to try to give an objective, God's-eye-view, description of the world. And the claim of what might be called *perspectivalism* is that this isn't possible.

Has metaphysics survived these three thrusts?

I think that it certainly has. The last three decades of the twentieth century saw a pretty remarkable rebirth of metaphysics. I'm not sure exactly when the resurgence began. Perhaps 1959, with the publication of Peter Strawson's *Individuals*, which he describes as an essay in descriptive metaphysics.

The reason it has survived is partly to do with the problems that we've already touched upon. Logical positivism, and indeed, perspectivalism, seem to be self-defeating. As for ordinary language philosophy, it is now seen to be sterile. It offers to dissolve all philosophical problems, and although that might have seemed exciting at the time, it was always unlikely that philosophers were going to adopt a procedure which proposes to destroy philosophy as a mode of enquiry.

Also, going back to logical positivism for a moment, the way that metaphysics is done now is very different from the way it was done at the end of the nineteenth century. Ayer was attacking these great cosmic visions, and perhaps he was right to do so. But looking at techniques of modern metaphysics, they actually more or less obey the logical positivist injunction.

Is it the case then that metaphysicians are pretty much agreed about the domain of the subject and its methodology? Or are there, for example, broad geographical variations in the way that the subject is pursued? The thought here is that perhaps British metaphysicians are less inclined to scientism than their American and Australian counterparts, and also much less inclined towards the kind of speculative metaphysics that is practised by philosophers in continental Europe?

I think it would be probably harder to discern something distinctive about British metaphysics (or views about metaphysics) now than it would have been say fifty years ago. And this is partly because fifty years ago you had about twenty British philosophy departments, of which only a handful were active and dominant. But now you have more than twice that number of departments, all of which are pretty active, so there's more work going on. Inevitably that means greater diversity.

Also, there has been quite a lot of movement between countries: quite a few people from abroad have been appointed to British posts – many more so in the last ten or fifteen years than was the case fifty years ago.

But I think your point about science is a pertinent one. I think British metaphysicians are fiercely defensive about the autonomy of metaphysics. It may be influenced by science, but it is not going to be dictated to by science.

I've also got a suspicion that British philosophers have perhaps a greater tendency towards what Strawson called 'descriptive metaphysics' over 'revisionary metaphysics'. Descriptive metaphysics is an attempt to provide a more detailed and precise conception of the world, but one that is suggested by our ordinary conceptions. Revisionary metaphysics, on the other hand, challenges our ordinary conceptual scheme. Certainly you have revisionary metaphysicians among the British crowd, but nevertheless one notices a certain metaphysical conservatism in people like Strawson, Richard Swinburne and Jonathan Lowe.

And what about the difference between Anglo-American metaphysics and the kind of speculative metaphysics done in continental Europe?

They're quite different. Certainly British philosophy continues to be dominated by the analytic method, by which I mean an interest in conceptual analysis, a concentration on argument, detection of inconsistency – things which I think are less important in the continental tradition.

Turning now more specifically to your own work, perhaps the area that you've written most frequently about is that of the nature of time. Yet, in terms of common-sense notions, there doesn't really seem to be a problem of time. We think there is a time of the present, which is now; a past which has gone, and is closed; and a future which is yet to come, and is relatively open. And I suppose we see time as being analogous to an inexorably flowing river. So what kind of thoughts do philosophers have that make the notion of time problematic?

In fact, I think it is precisely the dividing up of time into a past, present and future that is the key to many of the problems with time. Consider the past first – is the past real or not? I think we feel torn about this. On the one hand, we think it isn't real, that it's gone, it's just not here any longer. On the other hand, if it were completely unreal, then there would be nothing to make true our statements about the past – for example, the fact that the battle of Trafalgar took place on a certain date. If the past isn't real – if there are no past facts - what makes statements of that kind true or false?

I suspect that a lay person's answer to this conundrum would be something like this: the past did exist, it was real, there was a matter of fact about it, but it doesn't exist any more.

I think this leads to further problems. For example, as you said earlier, we do think of the past as being closed in the sense that we think that there is a matter of fact about it. But we think that the future is open, that there isn't a matter of fact about the future, it's all up for grabs. And yet although the future isn't yet real, one can think that it will be real, just as the past was once real. So why is the one open and the other closed? Simply saying that the past did happen whereas the future hasn't happened yet doesn't seem to explain that fundamental asymmetry between the two.

And if the future is to be thought of as real, does that mean that it is there waiting for us to discover it, or do we make the future? If it is, in some sense, already there waiting for us to discover it, then do we actually have any freedom at all, or is it already fixed what I shall do tomorrow?

Philosophers distinguish between A-theories of time and B-theories of time. What do they mean when they talk in this way?

The A-theory regards our intuitive distinction of time into a past, present and future as objective – as something which is quite independent of our experience of time. So it's quite independent of any mind or consciousness. If there were no sentient creatures in the universe, then there would still be a fact of the matter about what time is present. A-theorists also take the idea of the flow of time seriously. And most A-theorists, though by no means all, would think of the future as unreal and as open.

B-theorists, on the other hand, think that this division of time into past, present and future just reflects our perspective. So the distinction between past and present is no more significant metaphysically than the spatial distinction between what's here and what's there. Some B-theorists express this by saying that the division of time into past, present and future is mind-dependent. They say that there is no flow of time, and all times are equally real.

In your book *Arguing for Atheism*, you say some interesting things about the implications of these theories for our fear of death. What sort of thoughts did you have?

If you're an A-theorist, you take seriously the notion that time flows. It then seems that we spend our time hurtling towards oblivion. If you're a B-theorist, we're not doing this, we're not moving towards a state of non-existence. When we die, the world is not moving away from us. Reality is not going to leave us behind in this realm of non-existence. It is simply that we occupy a certain stretch of time, just as we occupy a certain volume of space. Death is just one of the temporal limits of our life. And as Lucretius once put it, our non-existence after death seems no more significant than our non-existence before our birth, and no one seems particularly exercised by the thought that we didn't exist before our births.

Why isn't that thought also a comfort if you're an A-theorist?

Maybe it depends crucially on how you view the reality of the past. There are certain A-theorists, sometimes called *presentists*, who think of the past as being as unreal as the future. In their view, reality really does leave us behind once we die. And the thought of being unreal is arguably quite a disturbing thought. Whereas for the B-theorist who thinks that all times are equally real, we remain just as real after our deaths as we were beforehand.

So it's just that B-theories remove the thought that we are inexorably pursuing our own unreality?

Yes. If you use the metaphor of the God's eye view, so you're looking down on the whole of time, there is a sense in which it is not objectively true that you are definitely dead. It is only objectively true that you occupy this stretch of time, and not these other stretches of time. There was a very famous book published in the 1930s by J. W. Dunn, called *An Experiment with Time*, and in this he expounds something that looks quite similar to a B-theory of time. Significantly, the title of one of his later books is *Nothing Dies*.

Shifting focus, what prompted you to write *Arguing for Atheism*? I'm wondering about this, because it is sometimes said that arguments about the traditional attempts to prove the existence of God are past their sell-by date.

I don't agree that the arguments are not interesting. I think there are two ways of looking at these traditional arguments. One is to see them as intended to be knock-down proofs of the existence of God. I think many people would say that they aren't. They're too problematic. They're either invalid or you can question one or other of the various premises. So they're very definitely not knock-down arguments.

But even if you concede that, it seems to me that they don't thereby lose their interest, because they can still be seen as challenges to the atheist. The theist is, in effect, saying: 'All right, I haven't got conclusive proof that God exists, but I can explain some things that you can't'.

So take the cosmological argument, the argument that there must be a first cause of everything, namely, God. You could attack that argument by saying that it is perfectly intelligible to suppose that the universe didn't have a beginning in time, that it's always existed. Or that it did have a beginning, but that it just popped into existence from nothing. If those are coherent descriptions, then we're not forced to believe in the existence of a first cause. On the other hand, the existence of the universe is nevertheless mysterious on the atheist view. So although the cosmological argument may fail as a knock-down proof, it remains as a challenge.

So one of the main reasons for writing the book was to see whether or not atheists can meet this kind of explanatory challenge, whether the demand for explanation is illegitimate, or whether the theist's explanation is in fact no explanation at all.

One of the interesting ideas that you explored in the book is the possibility that it might be possible to reconstruct theism along instrumentalist, or non-realist, lines; that is, that it is possible to view religious language as not making any kind of truth-claims. How does this argument work?

I suggested that there are basically three different positions that a theist can adopt. One is realism, which takes theological statements to be true, and for the most part holds that they should be taken literally. There may be certain areas where the language has to be interpreted metaphorically, but nevertheless, there are theological doctrines that have to be taken at face value, as describing something beyond the human mind.

The second position I called theological positivism. It takes theological statements to be true, but doesn't take them at face value. They have to be decoded. So theological statements, according to the positivists, are really coded propositions about morality – about the way one should live one's life, or the kinds of ideals that one should have. It should be possible, if positivism is right, to paraphrase statements that appear to be about a transcendent reality into statements about human nature, ideals and aspirations.

Theological instrumentalism, the third position that a theist can adopt, doesn't go in for paraphrase. It takes theological statements at face value. It's not trying to translate them into something else. But crucially, it takes them as being neither true nor false, so it's a non-realist position. Essentially, it treats theology as fiction.

Am I right in thinking that what's crucial for theological instrumentalism is the fact that religious language, though being analogous to fiction, is useful?

Yes, that's right. Presumably an atheist could see theological discourse as being fictional, but it would be a fiction that we can do without. Theological instrumentalists, on the other hand, would say that the fiction has a crucial point. Just as the scientific instrumentalist takes scientific statements to be neither true nor false, but nevertheless useful predictors of the outcome of certain experiments, so theological discourse and practices enable us to lead better lives, even though they are fictional.

Isn't there a danger for non-realist theism, that despite the claims of its advocates – for example, Don Cupitt – that it's a fictional discourse, it is in fact almost inevitably taken as comprising truth-claims? That is worrying both if you have a commitment to the value of truth and also because a lot of awful things are done in the name of religious belief.

I think it is indisputable that religious views have led to appalling atrocities. Crimes have been committed in the name of religion. But the instrumentalist will say that this shows you the dangers of a realist interpretation of religion. If people believe that they have access to the absolute truth, they may become intolerant and oppressive, whereas the instrumentalist would never commit these atrocities in the name of religion.

But if you're an instrumentalist, you're doing more than simply articulating a philosophical position. You have the thought that the rituals that go along with religious practice are desirable, and so on. However, there's a lot of research that suggests that people get seduced by ritual, so whatever might be claimed about the status of religious language, the suspicion must be that for psychological reasons people won't be able to avoid believing and acting as if the fictions they espouse are actually statements about matters of fact. And religious discourses are frequently predicated on exclusionary relations – they often divide up the world into the righteous and the unrighteous. Surely, whatever the status ascribed to religious language by non-realist theists, this is a worry?

That's a very interesting argument. As you say, people do get caught up in fictions. In fact, they get too caught up in fictions – they can be lost in the world of the fiction. But it would be surprising if someone, without actually losing contact with the thought that this is just a fiction, became intolerant of people who didn't want to join in.

Perhaps briefly we can look at the relationship between metaphysics and science. Is it possible to say anything general about their relationship?

There is a view, and I expect it is prevalent amongst scientists, that metaphysics is just proto-science. It's what people did before science came along. There is some truth in that. If you look at early metaphysical discussions in, for example, the work of Aristotle, then you can see that science has developed from those metaphysical enquiries.

But it is certainly wrong to say that science makes metaphysics redundant. It seems to me that at some level you can't do theoretical science without engaging in metaphysical issues. Suppose, for example, a physicist says that because we have conclusive evidence that there was a big bang, we know that time had a beginning. That would be to build in metaphysical assumptions. Who's to say that the beginning of the universe coincides with the beginning of time? Who's to say that nothing happened before the Big Bang? You can't generate these kinds of conclusions without building in some metaphysics in the first place. I think then that science and metaphysics are going to be intertwined with one another.

You conclude *Arguing for Atheism* with the thought that metaphysical commitments can, on certain readings, be equivalent to religious commitments. Is metaphysics any the worse for that?

Not at all. I meant by this simply that metaphysical views could have an impact on one's life, that they aren't simply dry abstract puzzles. So, for example, some of the puzzles that I was concerned with as a child, about the self, time and so on, aren't just intellectual paradoxes. They're something that people really care about.

And is metaphysics the field within which you are going to continue working?

Yes: metaphysics, philosophy of religion, and the intersection between the two. I'm currently working on the connections between metaphysical views of time – whether time really flows, whether it is independent of events in time, and so on – on the one hand, and the psychology of time on the other: How do we perceive time? What is going on when we remember things? I'm also intrigued by the notion of nothingness – perhaps this is my early interest in Sartre reasserting itself: What is it to say that something *doesn't* exist? Could there have been nothing at all rather than something? How can the *absence* of something be a cause of something else? Finally, I would like to tackle one of the most extraordinary and dramatic metaphysical propositions in religion: that God became man. Now there's an idea which is bound to connect up with fundamental issues about time, space and the self.

Select Bibliography

'Continuants and continuity', *The Monist*, 83, 2000

'Can beliefs be caused by their truth-makers?', *Analysis*, 59, 1999

'Time and the static image', *Philosophy*, 72, 1997

Arguing for Atheism: An Introduction to Philosophy of Religion, Routledge, 1996

Change, Cause and Contradiction: A Defence of the Tenseless Theory of Time, Macmillan, 1991

11 Continental Philosophy and Emancipation
In conversation with Simon Critchley

On the tomb of Karl Marx you will find the following inscription, taken from one of his *Theses on Feuerbach*: 'The Philosophers have only interpreted the world in various ways; the point however is to change it'. The first part of this statement reflects a commonplace idea about philosophy – that it is primarily an abstract and self-referential enterprise, which has little to say about people's lives and the social and political circumstances in which they are lived. The second part suggests that philosophy is at least somewhat the worse for this fact.

To the extent that philosophy is detached from the various concerns that characterise people's lives – whether these concerns be existential, social or political – it is a largely historically and culturally specific phenomenon. It is often seen as a mark of a certain kind of Anglo-American philosophy, but it is not true of philosophy as a whole. For example, central to ancient Greek philosophy was a concern with ethics and the conduct of life. Or, to give a radically different example, in present day China, philosophers have had some input into the 'One China Policy' with respect to Taiwan, and have also helped to theorise the new economic policies.

According to Simon Critchley, it is one of the *defining* characteristics of the tradition in philosophy that has come to be known as 'continental philosophy' that it is thoroughly engaged with social and political reality. The goal of continental philosophy is both individual and social emancipation.

If one thinks about some of the major figures who are grouped under the rubric of continental philosophy, then it is quite easy to discern this emancipatory agenda. The case of Karl Marx – the exemplary revolutionary thinker – is interesting. It is arguable whether all of Marx's oeuvre can be properly classified as philosophy. Whilst his early work was undoubtedly the result of an engagement with the ideas of Hegel and the young Hegelians, his later work is more in the line of critical, political economy. Nevertheless, his influence on the landscape of continental philosophy is undeniable. For example, his ideas have been more than incidentally important for thinkers as diverse as Georg Lukács, Max Horkheimer, Theodor Adorno, Herbert Marcuse, Jean-Paul Sartre, Maurice Merleau-Ponty, Louis Althusser, Pierre Bourdieu and Antonio Gramsci.

The contrast here with the situation in Anglo-American philosophy is striking. It is probably fair to say that there is no philosopher of the last 200 years of comparable influence. Moreover, it seems certain that a philosopher who placed the idea of revolutionary *praxis* (human activity or action) at the centre of their philosophy could never have played a comparable role in the Anglo-American tradition. Whilst it is probably too simplistic to claim that there is no sense of social or political engagement in Anglo-American philosophy, it is clear that any commitment of this kind is not at the centre of things in this tradition.

A concern with social and political emancipation is not the end of the story as far as emancipation and continental philosophy are concerned. There is also the issue of individual emancipation. Here Freud is perhaps the most important figure. His interest, at least initially, was to develop a technique – which turned out to be psychoanalysis – that could be used to alleviate the suffering associated with hysteria. Freud's was a limited emancipatory vision, since, in his view, psychoanalysis could only return people to a normal level of human suffering. For him, human misery is part and parcel of the human condition. However, his ideas were taken up and given wider scope by other thinkers. For example, Herbert Marcuse utilised a concept of 'surplus-repression' to argue that the domination of the ruling class was partly rooted in the unconscious. He claimed that social revolution would free up libidinal energy, and thereby produce a happier and calmer human society.

It would, of course, be possible to tell many different stories about continental philosophy. For example, one could look at the emergence of postmodernist philosophy in the work of thinkers like Jacques Lacan, Michel Foucault, Gilles Deleuze and Jacques Derrida. However, whatever story one told, one would still find a concern with philosophy as a critical, engaged activity. It is this that leads Simon Critchley to claim that the basic conceptual map of the continental tradition can be summarised in three terms: *critique, praxis* and *emancipation.*

It's not unusual amongst those people working in what might be termed continental philosophy that they came to the subject via an interest in literature. Was this the case with you?
Yes, I came to the University of Essex in 1982 to do English and European literature, because at the time I was obsessed with modernism and aspired to be a poet. The problem was that I wasn't a very good poet. When I got to university I became very disillusioned by the teaching of literature and literary theory. At the same time, I was doing a philosophy course, and I came to the conclusion that the people teaching philosophy were simply a lot smarter than the people who were teaching me literature, politics, French or sociology. I became intrigued, and

over the course of that year I switched to philosophy. At that point I had the enormous good fortune to be taught by some wonderful philosophers, all of whom seemed to have lots of time to talk with humble undergraduates: Robert Bernasconi, Jay Bernstein, Onora O'Neill, Frank Cioffi and others. It was and still is a great department.

What kind of thing had you been reading prior to coming to university?

I had a Penguin modern classics education! So I read Nietzsche extensively, and then heaps of moody modernist fiction. Sartre, Camus and Kafka were hugely important for me (Kafka still is), as were Joyce, Beckett and Flann O'Brien. And I developed a very early interest in existentialism. Then when I realised that one of the things that I could study at university was philosophy, I began to read the inevitable – you know, Russell's *Problems of Philosophy*, Ayer's *Central Questions of Philosophy*. If I'm honest, I didn't really get an enormous amount out of them.

So have you always had more sympathy for continental thinkers rather than analytical thinkers?

I think so, yes. For me philosophy has to address the question of existential commitment, and the fact that the person who is philosophising is a flesh and blood human being. It also has to address historical, social and political questions. It always seemed to me from very early on that what I learnt to call continental philosophy seemed to fit those concerns much better than Anglo-American philosophy. Of course, there are some exceptions. The later Wittgenstein has been an abiding interest of mine, and the M.Phil. thesis I wrote in France was a detailed comparative study of Heidegger and Carnap.

In broad terms, how would you draw a distinction between these two traditions in philosophy?

Well, there is more than one way to make the distinction, but my way is to take it back to Kant. I don't think continental philosophy makes much sense without its nineteenth century context, and particularly the work of Hegel and Nietzsche, so you do need to go back at least this far. Interesting and helpful as it is – and this is Michael Dummett's strategy in *Origins of Analytical Philosophy* – it is no good beginning in the late nineteenth century with Husserl and Frege.

There are two ways of reading Kant. There is an epistemological reading of Kant, which is overwhelmingly concerned with the success of the argument of the transcendental deduction and how Kant responds or fails to respond to Humean scepticism. If one begins from this reading of Kant, then you end up with the way in which Kant continues to be taken up in the Anglo-American world.

The other way of reading Kant, which is the way that dominates the continental tradition, is in terms of the problems set in the *Third Critique*. It was felt by post-Kantians like Maimon and Jacobi, and by the German idealists, that Kant had established a series of dualisms in the *Third Critique* – pure reason and practical reason, nature and freedom, epistemology and ethics – but had failed to provide a single unifying principle which would bring those dualisms together. German idealism, then, can be seen as a series of attempts to provide this principle. So you get the Subject in Fichte, Spirit in Hegel, art in the early Schelling, and then in later nineteenth and early twentieth century German philosophy, Will to Power in Nietzsche, Praxis in Marx and Being in Heidegger. These are all attempts to answer this question.

The other thing to add is that the real core issue in the continental, post-Kantian tradition is a question which has the following form, which is first raised by Hamann: If there is to be a critique of reason of the Kantian form, then surely reason has to criticise itself. And if reason has to criticise itself, how does one stop the critique of reason ending in total scepticism? So, in my view, the problem that has animated the continental tradition from the very early nineteenth century onwards, from Jacobi to be precise, is the threat of *nihilism*. This is the threat that everything that is solid will melt into the air, that the highest values – like truth, justice or whatever – have somehow devalued themselves. Continental philosophy from the post-Kantians up to philosophically opposed figures like Heidegger and Adorno can best be seen as a series of responses to nihilism.

The suggestion here is that reason itself – the motor of the Enlightenment project – throws into doubt the very ground upon which it stands. Is the imperative to think through existential commitment, political commitment, and so on, in part related to this consequence of the enlightenment project?

The basic problem here is what Adorno and Horkheimer call 'the dialectic of enlightenment'. That is, enlightenment, the belief in the supremacy of reason and human rationality, undergoes historically an inversion which leads to its opposite, namely the barbarism of Auschwitz. That, as it were, the defence of reason and enlightenment somehow risks conspiring with a nihilism which seems to undermine all that is of value.

For continental philosophers, this is both a philosophical problem and a *sociohistorical* problem. So another difference between analytical and continental philosophy would consist in the fact that from Hegel onwards, systematic philosophical questions have to be linked to socio-historical enquiry. From this point of view, the distinctions between philosophy, history and society begin to fall apart. In that sense, the question becomes: Given the enlightenment defence of the supremacy of reason, how does one begin to explain what actually happened, from the violences of colonialism, the world wars, the gulag, through to Bosnia and Rwanda?

So does this explain why amongst continental philosophers – I'm thinking of people like Marx, Freud and Habermas – there is a critical, emancipatory agenda?

Yes! In my view, the basic conceptual map of the continental tradition can be summarised in three terms: *critique, praxis* and *emancipation*. And I think that what unifies philosophers in the continental tradition is a concern with philosophy as a critical activity in the Kantian sense, which is a critique both of dogmatic metaphysics, but also a critique of existing social reality and existing praxis. The goal of philosophy in the continental tradition is emancipation, whether individual or societal.

There is perhaps something worrying about this idea of social engagement in that social engagement is not necessarily directed towards ends that one might find desirable. Consider, for example, Heidegger's commitment to National Socialism. Isn't there a worry then that if philosophers are socially engaged, they are going to be engaged in projects that one finds unpalatable?

There is that worry. And there are many examples of philosophers defending stupid or evil courses of action. As you know, Frege was a vociferous anti-Semite. On the continental side, there is no question to my mind that Heidegger's philosophy and his politics are linked, and that, for him, there is an intrinsic connection between his account of individual and collective authenticity in *Being and Time*, and his commitment to National Socialism in 1933. Sartre said many questionable things in support of many causes, but also took heroically principled positions particularly on questions of race. So continental philosophers have made mistakes. Foucault defended the Iranian revolution. That has led some people, particularly people working in French intellectual history, to question the whole category of the intellectual – the philosophically informed commentator on everyday life. So the argument would be that given that philosophers have got their commitments wrong, then they shouldn't be committed in that way, but should be concerned with their professional business and stay out of politics. I disagree with that most vigorously, I think there are plenty of counter-examples of philosophers defending good causes. Exemplary in this regard is a figure like Habermas whose journalistic interventions have been crucial in shaping German popular opinion for a generation. I also think that Derrida's political positions on pedagogical reform in France and his support for a wide variety of causes have been a good thing. To my mind, we need philosophers to be more concerned with public intellectual issues and less obsessed with their professional esteem.

Perhaps the worry for those looking at continental philosophy from the outside has to do with the relatively unsophisticated, but nevertheless commonplace, idea that continental philosophers all buy into the notion that truth is relative to discourse, and that therefore in this tradition any thoughts about the ethics of a particular political intervention will occur entirely within the bounds of the particular philosophical schema embraced by the philosopher advocating the intervention.

I think the continual misapprehension about continental philosophy is the question of relativism. On my account, continental philosophy begins in the 1790s with Jacobi's thought that the Kantian critique of reason might open up the floodgates to relativism by making all experience of reality subject-dependent and therefore subject-relative.

So the continental tradition to my mind is concerned at least in part with *responding* to the threat of relativism, and responding to it in some cases by defending universalism. This paradox is at its clearest in a thinker like Derrida, who is always perceived as a relativist, and yet from the beginning a consistent thread in his philosophical position has been the critique of relativism. He picks up this critique from Husserl. In Derrida's later work, we see him moving more and more explicitly towards a defence of a normative universalism, and a belief in the undeconstructability of justice, as he puts it, which is an overarching value that cannot be relativised. I think this situation is typical of a whole strand of continental philosophy, so in that sense continental philosophy is premised on the threat of relativism, and the desire to counter that threat through producing a philosophy that is critically rigorous and linked, furthermore, to a notion of human emancipation.

I take the point about Derrida, but it is possible to point to other continental thinkers, for example, Bruno Latour, or certain readings of Foucault – as for example in *Discipline and Punish,* where he appears to be a long way from thinking that the ending of barbaric punishment is a good thing – where relativism does seem to be a recognisable theme. Also, one can point to the way in which continental philosophy has been adopted in the English speaking world, particularly perhaps in literary and critical theory, where people do actually seem to embrace a thoroughgoing relativism. Is that not a worry?

Yes it is. But I think that people who adopt this kind of relativism are guilty of a misapprehension that is based on historical amnesia. Part of the job that I see myself doing is reminding people of the nature of philosophical modernity and its abiding relevance. Thinkers like Derrida and Habermas are best understood in relationship to a particular story in the last two hundred years, coming out of the Kantian tradition.

So I think the relativism accusation is a misapprehension, and universalism is at least a site of conflict, and in my view is something that has to be defended. However, there are philosophers in the continental tradition who are relativists, Baudrillard for example. In that sense I'm not defending the whole tradition, but giving that tradition a certain construction, a certain spin. There are significant parts of the continental tradition that have argued for positions that I think are uninteresting, indefensible or simply wrong.

I want to move on to the issue of nihilism. In your *Continental Philosophy*, you say that you have your own thoughts about how one responds to the problem of nihilism, but you didn't go into any detail. What kind of thoughts, then, do you have about nihilism?

Nihilism, for Nietzsche, is the devaluation of the highest values. This can also be thought of in relation to his expression *God is dead*. The highest value, God, has become devalued. It has become something in which we can no longer believe.

The originality of Nietzsche's insight is that the death of God is something brought about by human progress. That's why the madman says *God is dead. We have killed him*. So, the period of history that we call modernity leads to the death of God, the devaluing of the highest values. The question then raised is that if the highest values have been devalued, how are they to be revalued? Given that we have lost the Platonic/Christian plot with respect to the answer to the question of the meaning of life, how do we answer it for ourselves?

Nietzsche's thought is overwhelmingly concerned with how one responds to the historical and philosophical situation of nihilism. And his response, I think, is given with the concept of eternal return. If one can accept the sheer meaninglessness of the universe and affirm that thought, over and over again, then one is equal to the meaninglessness of the universe, and one no longer falls into despair. So the superman or, better, *overman* is the person who is capable of sustaining the thought of eternal recurrence without embracing some new idol.

So that is one response to nihilism, but my thought is somewhat different. I think that the Nietzschean model of nihilism, and the affirmation of eternal return, is too *heroic*, too solitary, and too distant from the grain and detail of everyday life. In my book, *Very Little, Almost Nothing*, I try to show that there are four responses to nihilism in the philosophical and literary tradition, and that they're all wrong, in one way or another. And I come up with a fifth response to nihilism, which I can only summarise in terms of certain formulae.

If nihilism is the threat of the collapse of meaning, then my position is that one has to accept meaninglessness as an *achievement*, as an accomplishment that permits a transformed relation to everyday life. So, in many ways, my response to nihilism is the acceptance of the meaninglessness of big metaphysical answers to the problem of life which is precisely not a counsel of despair, but rather a call back to the ordinary, to the obvious, but often enigmatic, grain and detail of everyday life. There are several thinkers that I try to bring to bear on that thought, most notably Stanley Cavell. But the anti-heroic hero of my response to nihilism is Samuel Beckett, and, in a long discussion of the *Trilogy*, I try to show how this orientation to the ordinary does not lead to a tragic world view, but rather to comedy, to the wry, mocking, sardonic smiles of Beckett's humour: Clov to Hamm in *Endgame*, 'Do you believe in the life to come?' Hamm to Clov, 'Mine was always that'.

You say something interesting about the modern progressive reaction to nihilism, which is that it is 'methodologically characterised

by a belief in the reciprocal fertility of philosophy and sociology'.
What do you take the modern progressive reaction to nihilism to
be? And, in general terms, do you think that philosophy stands to
gain by incorporating the methods and ideas of other disciplines?

I try to argue that there are two ways of following up the Nietzschean
thought of nihilism, and those two ways I call *progressive* and *reactionary* modernism. The two responses take the following form: The
reactionary nihilist, like Heidegger, Spengler and maybe Wittgenstein,
would interpret modern Western culture from the perspective of
philosophy, and would find that culture wanting, because it is decadent,
dumbed down, not informed by the summits of European culture.
And from this lofty, eagle's nest viewpoint comes the suspicion of
democracy, equality and the rest. That's reactionary nihilism.

Progressive modernism would be another way of hearing the
Nietzschean thought, and it holds that the task of the philosopher is to
respond to the situation of meaninglessness by defending human
emancipation, by upholding the ideals of the Enlightenment despite
their deformation in the modern world, despite the Gulag and the
Holocaust. And that's the tradition that you can find in Weber, and in
the Frankfurt School.

The question that you raise about the relationship of philosophy to
other disciplines is an interesting one. For the Frankfurt School, philosophy is the name of a problem, not just the name of a solution to a
problem. Philosophy is a discourse of conceptual abstraction, which, as
it were, conspires with the abstraction of labour and commodification
in capitalist society. So, for the Frankfurt School, philosophy is part of
the intellectual and social edifice that is blocking emancipation. It follows that philosophical categories have to be linked to social analysis,
and vice versa, sociological analysis has to be philosophically informed.
This means that philosophy without sociological, empirical insight is

empty. And if one judges society from a solely philosophical perspective, one ends up in a situation of being a reactionary modernist. Of course, it also means that sociology without philosophy is blind.

So another thing which is distinctive about the continental tradition is the way in which philosophy is deemed impoverished in different ways. And philosophical questions have to be linked to non-philosophical discourses. It's almost axiomatic in the continental tradition that philosophy will be linked to things outside of itself, whether this is the aesthetic in early Schelling and German romantics, Christianity in Kierkegaard, political economy in Marx, psychoanalysis in Freud, and so on.

So what do you think lies behind any reluctance on the part of analytical philosophy to embrace subjects outside itself? Do you think it might have something to do with the way that professionalisation occurred?

Although philosophy, since its inception in Plato, has always been linked to the academy, to more or less formal schools of thought, the professionalisation of philosophy is a recent phenomenon. And I think it's a lamentable phenomenon. Just visit the Eastern Division annual meeting of the American Philosophical Association for an empirical confirmation of this thesis – it's a meat market! To a certain extent, this professionalism insulates philosophers from other disciplines and encourages a certain lazy arrogance. What I dislike most about philosophers is the idea that they think because they are smart as philosophers they have nothing to learn from anybody else. You find this repeatedly. I'd argue that they've got lots to learn, not just from cognitive scientists, but from lawyers, historians, anthropologists and sundry others. If philosophy isolates itself from other disciplines and from the culture at large it will die, and furthermore it would not have deserved to live anyway. If philosophy does not do more to open itself up to other conversations, then it risks going out of business.

Changing tack slightly, part of your commitment to phenomenological method, to a concern with human subjects and human intersubjectivity, seems to be that it offers a way to overcome the problem of what you call 'scientism'. What do you take this problem to be?

I think there are two pernicious tendencies in philosophy and also in culture more generally, which I want to call 'scientism' and 'obscurantism'. Scientism is the belief that all phenomena can be explained through the methodology of the natural sciences, and the belief that, therefore, all phenomena are capable of a causal explanation. This is a tendency that is obviously endemic in a scientific culture like Britain, and it also dominates professional philosophy through the various programmes of naturalisation. So one threat, and one thread, within contemporary philosophy is scientism.

Obscurantism is precisely a reaction against the predominance of scientific explanation in the public sphere. Obscurantism is both an intellectual worry, and a cultural worry. What happens is that one understandable but misguided reaction to a science-dominated culture is the rejection of science. This is what I call the X-Files complex. People feel that science tries to explain everything, but this is wrong, and it has to be rejected, because the truth is out there, but it is not in a form that science can causally explain. In every X-Files programme, there are two lines of explanation, one line is causal-scientific, the other is also causal, but it is an obscure causal line. In the X-Files it is always the obscure cause that is shown to be right, but in some way we cannot fully understand. It's a mystery.

Thus, I think there is a cultural tendency, as a reaction to scientism, to throw science away, and to embrace obscurantism. So my pathology of contemporary philosophy – although this is obviously something of a caricature – is that, at its worst, there is a tendency towards scientism in analytic philosophy, and in a counterbalancing way, there is a tendency towards obscurantism in continental philosophy. What I mean is that in continental philosophy, there is a tendency to explain everything in terms of 'one big thing' that pretends to have some causal or causal-sounding efficacy. So you've got 'the death drive' in Freud, 'being' in Heidegger, 'the real' in Lacan, 'power' in Foucault, 'the other' in Levinas, '*différance*' in Derrida, and there are other examples. This is a pernicious tendency in my view. There is no one big thing, just many small things, fascinating small things, which it is the job of phenomenology to describe.

What I want to argue for, then, is a version of continental philosophy that does not have to embrace a 'one big thing' obscurantism. This is a line of thought one can find in the later Husserl, and which influenced Heidegger and Merleau-Ponty. Husserl's last manuscript was *The Crisis of the European Sciences*, and what he meant by 'crisis' was the crisis of scientism or what he called 'objectivism', the idea that you can explain everything that there is by finding the objective causes behind the appearance, a technique not only applied to the external world, but, even more egregiously, to the human subject in scientific psychology. What Husserl thought was critically wrong about scientism was that it overlooked the subjective and intersubjective spheres, what he called the 'lifeworld'. The practices of the natural sciences are parasitic upon and secondary to life-world practices, and the latter cannot be naturalistically reduced to the former.

What both scientism and obscurantism overlook is simple social understanding, our pre-theoretical life in the world. And what social understanding requires is not causal or causal-sounding hypotheses, but rather a form of phenomenology. Phenomenology, on my rather minimal model, is concerned with the production of remarks which clarify and reorder the phenomena that we are presented with, producing aspect change with regard to things. This is a highly reactionary Wittgensteinian position, but it needs to be brought back to our attention because it happens to be true.

So phenomenology for me is a way of assembling reminders which clarify the social world in which we exist. It is a technique of redescription. The cultural problem is that we somehow don't feel that such a form of social explanation is enough and we seem to crave elaborate causal hypotheses, all sorts of 'big things' pulling the strings behind the scenes.

Moving to the present, what are you working on at the moment?

I am working quite hard on the early Heidegger at the moment and will try and turn that into a small book at some distant future point. But my main project is a book on humour with the imaginative title *On Humour* in which, odd as it sounds, I'm going to try to do some philosophy, rather than simply talking about it. My basic claim, which picks up on much that I've said in this conversation, is that humour provides an *oblique phenomenology of ordinary life*; it is a way of describing the situation of our existence and, at its best, it indicates how we might change that situation. Jokes are exemplary forms of reminders in the sense I just described.

Humour, for me, is practically enacted philosophy. It shows how often quite elaborate forms of reflection are embedded in everyday life. It is the ability to take a critical, reflective stance with regards to that life. To see social relationships and all practices for what they are, and to be able to imagine how they might otherwise be. So humour is an exemplary philosophical practice which is phenomenologically descriptive, critical and emancipatory. I think this is why Wittgenstein made the very serious remark that a book of philosophy could be written entirely in the form of jokes.

The other interesting thing about humour is that it is what I call a 'nicely impossible object'. You don't need a philosopher to tell you about humour. Perish the thought! So the point of the book is to indicate that we already know how this works, it just needs to be properly foregrounded. It is a question of making the implicit explicit. The important thing is to use specific examples of humour, and to let those examples do a lot of philosophical work, carry the weight of the argument without being burdened with too much theoretical baggage, whether they are examples of jokes, literary quotations, film stills or whatever. This means writing in a more direct way than I have attempted until now. I am certain that it will be an enormous success.

Select Bibliography

On Humour, Routledge, 2002

Continental Philosophy: A Very Short Introduction, Oxford University Press, 2001

Ethics–Politics–Subjectivity: Derrida, Levinas and Contemporary French Philosophy, Verso, 1998

A Companion to Continental Philosophy (editor), Blackwell, 1998

Very Little . . . Almost Nothing, Routledge, 1997

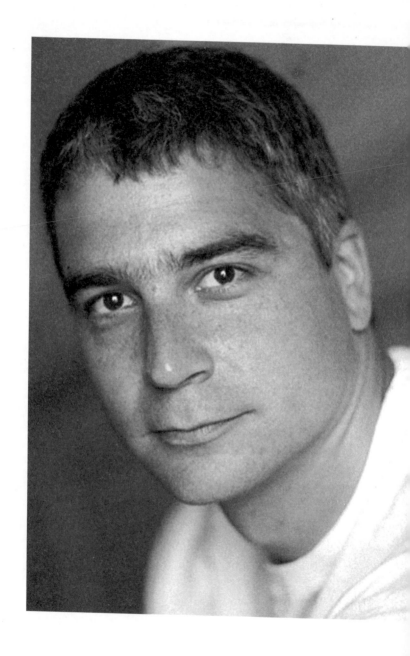

12   The Analytic and the Continental

In conversation with Simon Glendinning

A recent graduate in philosophy from a British university goes to mainland Europe for a possibly well-earned break. There she meets a German and a Frenchman and discovers that they too studied philosophy. Keen to engage her in conversation, the two foreigners start to talk about their favourite philosophers. The names they rattle off sound familiar: Heidegger, Husserl, Merleau-Ponty, Derrida, Kierkegaard, and so on. But the graduate is unable to discuss these philosophers with her new friends. 'I've heard a bit about them,' she explains (in English), 'but I've never actually studied them'.

So she tries to discuss her favourite philosophers. She talks about Russell, Ryle, Ayer, Strawson, Quine and Nagel. Her new friends are now as mute as she was. 'We've heard a bit about them,' they explain (in English), 'but we've never actually studied them'.

Finally, they find something they can talk about. Going back to the greats, they find they have all read Kant, Spinoza, Aristotle and Plato. They do have something in common, after all.

What does this encounter tell us about the state of philosophy in Europe today? It does reflect certain generally agreed facts about the differences between what we can call 'Anglo-Saxon' philosophy in Britain and 'continental' philosophy as studied in mainland Europe. The first such fact is that there is a big difference in which philosophers are most widely read, most notably among twentieth century thinkers. Continental philosophy's key figures are generally French or German, and include among their number phenomenologists, existentialists and post-structuralists. Anglo-Saxon philosophy's key figures are generally British and American and tend to be working in the broadly analytic tradition.

What the encounter also reflects is that both continental and Anglo-Saxon philosophy share a common heritage. Indeed, although the roots of the rift are usually traced back to the different responses to Kant, the rift itself only really became apparent in the last century. Before then, the idea of any kind of serious philosophical gulf between the two parts of Europe would have seemed implausible.

But beyond these historical and social facts about who reads what and who the key figures now are, the depth and importance of the division is a matter of debate. While some see the two traditions as pursuing essentially different subjects which both happen to be called 'philosophy', others argue that, fundamentally, there is little, if anything, of substance which divides them.

Simon Glendinning pitches his tent in the latter camp. His work draws on thinkers and problems from both traditions. For example, his book, *On Being with Others*, brings in the philosophy of Heidegger, Derrida and Wittgenstein to address a problem central to both traditions: the problem of other minds.

In the Anglo-Saxon tradition, the problem is usually framed as a sceptical doubt. To have a mind is to have a certain subjective perspective on the world. A person with a mind thinks, feels and senses. But thinking, feeling and sensing all seem to be essentially private. You cannot see what I'm thinking, feel what I'm feeling or experience exactly what I experience. In this way, the minds of others are closed to us.

But if this is the case, how do we know that others have minds at all? All we see are the behaviours which we take to be signs of an inner life. But just as an actor can pretend to be in pain while feeling no discomfort at all, or a robot could be programmed to 'laugh' even though it had no sense of humour, couldn't other people be displaying the signs of an inner life without actually having one?

Of course, no one is seriously suggesting that other people do not have minds, but the philosophical problem is how we rationally justify our belief that they do.

Glendinning's approach to this problem illustrates how he brings together the philosophers and problems of the Anglo-Saxon and continental traditions. It challenges those who believe that the divide between the two is deep and fundamental, and supports the case that more unites than divides them.

There is another divide which Glendinning has also tried to bridge: that between academic philosophy and the public. Through the Forum for European Philosophy, he has organised talks at the Hayward Gallery in London, where philosophers have given public lectures on substantive themes connected with a current exhibition. In this, as with the rest of his work, Glendinning has been concerned to make connections without 'dumbing down'.

Philosophers often talk about a distinction between analytic philosophy and continental philosophy. Over time, you've lost interest in the divide, in the sense that you don't think it reflects a real division in the subject. Why is this so? Where, if anywhere, do the real divisions lie?

There is a division within analytic philosophy between those who do and those who do not see philosophy as importantly continuous with natural science. I think that division can be seen within writings outside analytic philosophy too, and it cuts across the analytic and continental distinction, which ultimately lacks any deep philosophical significance. The crucial distinction is between those who do and those who do not see the possibility of an investigation which is both non-empirical and non-metaphysical. Heidegger described it in an essay as 'neither metaphysics nor science'. The authors I am most interested in are those who wish to affirm that possibility. It doesn't just so happen, but it is the case that authors working with that point of view come from both the analytic and continental camps.

Could you say what you mean when you say about a mode of investigation, that it's neither empirical nor metaphysical?

There's a way I could put it which is derived from Wittgenstein and Heidegger, which is that metaphysics is to be understood as the enquiry into the foundations of everything empirical, an enquiry into the essence of the world. So that would be a non-scientific investigation in an important respect, because it's not an investigation of some particular region of reality – the biological, chemical, physical or geographical, what Husserl calls the regional sciences, and what Heidegger calls the investigation into entities or beings – but rather it's an investigation into the essence of beings or the Being of beings. So metaphysics is the enquiry into the Being of beings, science the investigation of beings. To be neither metaphysics nor science means that you're neither going to be conducting an enquiry into the essence of beings nor are you going to investigate objects in some kind of empirical way. This leaves room for a variety of other kinds of philosophical enquiry. There are various ways of proceeding that could go by that name. But, let me add, the analytic/continental distinction won't be a significant way of sorting them out.

In a recent paper, you have said that your work 'is characterised by a commitment to the possibility of and need for a distinctively non-empirical inquiry, alongside appreciation of there being nothing more to "reality" than the (in principle) "everything" that is (in principle) open to scientific research'. So, in a sense, the rejection of the metaphysical side of philosophy can be put positively as an acceptance of the fact that all we have is the empirical reality of the world.

Yes, exactly.

Within the analytic tradition there's a lot of suspicion, or even worse, derision, about continental philosophy. You've got some particular ideas about what the source of this ill will is.

This is a difficult story because it's neither going to be simply a philosophical story about one kind of philosopher rejecting or refuting another kind, so that we could find clearcut intraphilosophical grounds for the division; nor is it simply sociohistorical – for example, a reflection of national, political or religious hostility between different thinkers or their cultural backgrounds. I do think that the distinction is basically historical and institutional, but that does not mean that the account of the growth of the distinction and division, the developing idea of a wide gulf, has no philosophical significance. Let me put my view of that rather boldly.

The basic view I have is that continental philosophy represents, for analytic philosophy, proper philosophy's own other. Historically, that position has been represented under the title of sophistry. So you have a contrast between philosophy and sophistry. I think most of the rhetoric of analytic philosophy's representation of the division deploys the kinds of evaluative distinctions you find when we talk about the distinction between philosophy and sophistry. You line things up between logic and rhetoric; clarity and obscurity; precision and vagueness; literal language and poetic language; analysis and speculation; and so on. This general other to philosophy is philosophy's own other – it's not, as it were, philosophy versus sociology, but philosophy versus what is philosophy's own other. What's been distinctive in the twentieth century is that what had already been called, in Britain at least, 'continental philosophy' took the position of that other.

Or perhaps we should say was given that position by people within the analytic tradition. That's not how it conceived itself.

No, it's not. Here we come to perhaps the most notable feature of this, which is that continental philosophy could not have conceived itself, because crudely speaking, there is no continental philosophy. The very term 'continental' is an Anglophone designation. The word belongs to the English language and designates the European mainland as distinct from the British Isles. So you had what we do and what they do. Unfortunately for the historian, what they do was not what we said they were doing, but nevertheless, the analytic movement, as it was conceiving its own identity, in part conceived itself through its difference to this other. Continental philosophy came to take the place of all that is to be avoided if you are to be doing proper philosophy.

This leaves continental philosophy as the title for a kind of construction, and so when you come to ask yourself, 'what is continental philosophy?', you don't find that there is anything which is continental philosophy or which belongs to a distinctive continental tradition of philosophy. You find that there are all kinds of movements there which have all sorts of connections with each other, as they also do with analytic philosophy. Of course, some are manifestly much closer to some analytic philosophy than others are, but then there are all kinds of movements within analytic philosophy too. There is no large scale or basic philosophical division of the kind that many would still like to find. Nevertheless, in the end, I think there is a way of articulating the distinction, but it will show why the oppositions that analytic philosophers have appealed to will never do the job. If we're looking for a definition of continental philosophy, I have this answer: it's the false personification by self-styled analytic philosophy of a possibility which is internal to and which threatens all philosophising – that is the possibility of being empty, the possibility of sophistry.

I think the great worry, the great tragedy as well, is that by externalising that possibility under the name 'continental philosophy', analytic philosophy has been able to think of itself as free of that possibility, which is a disaster, really. It's always a tricky moment for any philosopher to acknowledge that what you are doing, what you think might be worth doing, might be just a spinning in the wind or just a kind of doing nothing at all, or doing something very badly. I think one of the most unhelpful features of the idea of a wide gulf between analytic and continental philosophy is that it's allowed analytic philosophers to think of themselves as having freed themselves from something it is impossible to free yourself from.

I want to turn to your book *On Being with Others*. It deals with the traditional problem of other minds, which you think contains within it a misconception. The traditional problem is supposed to be a philosophical difficulty in justifying an attribution of mental states to other people. An anecdote and some allusions in the text made me wonder how much your unease with the traditional problem really stems from your relationships with the animals in your life. Is there something in that?

Yes, but there is a rather long route towards that because the problem of other minds, as represented in its traditional form, is about other persons, and it takes a long time for me to get to the point of thinking that the expression of a problem here is bound up with assumptions about the rigour of the boundary between the human and the non-human.

In one respect, the entry of animals into my work is simply of the form that what I say about the relationships between human beings is going to hold too for the relationships between human beings and other animals, and other animals and other animals. So the way I develop the problematic opens up the opportunity of thinking, not just about one's relationship to other human minds, but to other minds in general.

One way that comes through is that, *pace* the sceptic, we show no more hesitancy in attributing certain psychological states to certain other animals than we do in attributing certain psychological states to certain other human beings. I wanted to do justice to that, to the fact that our engagements with others in everyday life are not only engagements with other human beings, although obviously for most human beings today they are largely relations to other human beings. There is a deeper level at which, for me, the way in which animals figure in a work of philosophy tells you an awful lot about that philosopher's way of looking at things.

I was wondering how much this was a start or end point to the reflections in the book. For example, one theme is the rejection of what you call humanism, the view that there is something special about human beings – perhaps their subjectivity – that separates them from animals. You see that as being part of the framework within which the problem of other minds arises. It seems then that if you recognise the importance of relations with others, including non-human animals, but you see that humanism is essential to framing the problem, then before you've done any philosophy, you'll pretty much know the problem cannot have been framed correctly.

That's right, but there is still a good deal of philosophy to be done. Since I argue for a view which doesn't see a radical cut or break between human beings and other animals, that might seem to situate me with what are sometimes called naturalists. But it's not just humanism that I resist in the book, it's naturalism too – naturalism being the view that we are just animals and animals are just biological organisms. The humanist tendency has been to say that naturalism holds for animals, everything about their behaviour can be explained in biological terms, but it doesn't hold for human beings. We have this distinctive trait, for example, subjectivity or language or rationality. In the end, I want to say that the naturalistic definition doesn't even hold for animals. We can't see animals, not all animals at any rate, simply in terms of the behaviour of a biological organism. That's not because they too have some additional trait that we've been traditionally assigning to human beings alone. We've got to find a way of rethinking human animality – and animality in general – which avoids the humanist tendency to supply some extra trait to an animal organism or the naturalist tendency to reduce everything to the behaviour of biological organisms.

Your strategy is not to solve the problem of other minds, but to reframe it in such a way that the problem no longer arises. Can you explain how a strategy like that works?

The contrast is with a refutation. A refutation would aim to demonstrate, one way or another, that we do know what the sceptic doubts we know. We do have knowledge about the psychological states of other persons. A reframing wants to try to grasp why it is that human beings may come to find themselves trying to refute the sceptic.

The book is a fine-grained argument, so it's hard to isolate particular elements, but one idea which seems to be important is that of iterability. Could you explain what iterability means in its limited linguistic usage, before we look at how you broaden it out a bit?

Think about a person using language and look upon some occasion of their uttering something as an event of some kind. The idea of iterability is that this event, to be the event that it is, can't be described unless we include in that description a reference to another such event, that is, an event which isn't what *it* is except in virtue of its relationship to another such event, and so on. There is, in this description, an indefinite, continuous structure of reference to other such events. The point is not that numbers are constantly accumulating here, it's just that there's a limit of not once. In this discussion of iterability, the vocabulary comes from Derrida, but the idea is also found in Wittgenstein's asking if it is possible for one man, as he puts it, to obey a rule once, to which he says, not once. So in anything like an event of speech, the possibility of an iteration on some other occasion is internal to its being what it is.

The basic idea is that symbolism – structures of signs, language and symbols – has this iterative structure, rather than being, on the one hand, unique events, dateable singular occurrences, and on the other hand, ideal meanings, which are general and in a certain way timeless. I call that, following Derrida, thinking at once both the rule and the event, rather than splitting the phenomenon of language between, on the one hand, singular events, and on the other, general, ideal meanings.

To take an example, I say, 'the cat is sleeping over there'. On a naive view of language, what enables me to do that is that there are universal concepts like 'cat' and 'sleeping' which exist in some

timeless, Platonic realm and I'm helping myself to these universals on a specific occasion. Are you saying that it is rather that the particular utterance 'the cat is sleeping over there' is possible, because on other occasions it is possible to say the same or a similar thing?

That equivocation gets to the heart of it. The notion of iterability doesn't in any way jeopardise the notion of going on in the same way, but it does draw attention to the fact that this sameness doesn't exclude empirical differences which are manifest when we actually look at how we use these kinds of symbols. Wittgenstein illustrated this with the notion of family resemblance. When we talk about using a word in the same way, that doesn't mean there has to be one thing which is actually the same in every application. So we have to think about the use of language in a way which gives content to the notion of going on in the same way, without requiring of ourselves that we can identify or discover some aspect or element which is the same in every case. Iterability aims to capture both this sameness and this difference.

And also accounts for the possibility of the use of a word changing?
Yes. It's indefinitely open to future contingencies, which can't be circumscribed in advance.

One thing you do is extend the notion of iterability to human behaviour in general. How does that work?
Something like waving is a piece of behaviour which we can consider as an event. If we think about it as a movement of the arm, we could think of it purely naturalistically, that is to say, as the behaviour of a biological organism. But we might want to say a wave is not just that, it has some kind of symbolic dimension, and so we might then oscillate towards a humanist account of some kind where we say it's the

outward expression of some inner intention or conscious process which lies behind it. My hope is that the notion of iterability can cut between those two seemingly exhaustive alternatives by saying that this piece of behaviour is what it is only in virtue of its iterability. So we have an enriching of the description of the event which neither makes recourse to occult or spiritual entities or processes, nor just sees it as a piece of mere behaviour.

I want to see how far the notion of iterability can extend. The example you give of waving could be seen as a kind of quasi-linguistic activity, the giving of a symbol which on a naive view would be an expression of some inner thought or intention. But can you talk about iterability in the context of someone sitting ner-vously, for example? If someone is sitting nervously, they may not be actually thinking about anything in particular, and certainly not sitting in that way in order to indicate to anyone else how they feel – they may even be trying to cover it up. Does iterability extend to behaviours like that?

It does, although this is a difficult area because you're addressing issues of what I'd like to call the development or transformation of natural expressions. An example that Wittgenstein uses again and again is nat-ural and linguistic expressions of pain. In the case of a pre-linguistic child or an animal there will be a natural expression of the sensation, and that is already a behavioural syndrome. That is, it is a distinctive pattern of behaviour; a structure that, even prior to its appropriation in a symbolic culture, is not simply describable in terms of movements of a body on this occasion. So again, and from the start, I try to get iterability to give us a richer notion of behaviour through building into the description of the behaviour occasions other than the present one.

What would be important about someone sitting nervously – and this is the general form of the account I've given – is that in order for it to be an intelligible piece of behaviour, it must be possible for it to function in their absence, without their presence. So the piece of behaviour is not tied up so completely with their unique physiology that it couldn't be identified on some other occasion in somebody else. It is clearer in the case of signs and linguistic expressions that they can function in the absence of any given user.

Could you sketch out how this notion of iterability functions as at least part of the way of avoiding scepticism about other minds?

First of all we have this idea that iterability brings in not only other occasions but the possibility of functioning in one's radical absence, by another. This means that for the most part our behaviour has this structural relation to others. So we have here a position where it's not a question of sharing knowledge of rules, but being engaged in a practice in which a relation to others is built into it, from the start. I've called this a structural publicness to all uses of signs. This public language argument should serve to prevent a sceptical view about, for example, the functioning of language where I can never know what you mean, or a view on which the meaning of words is so dependent on my subjectivity that I can't tell if anyone means the same as me or means anything at all. We're getting a description of the structure and functioning of language where the sceptical view simply can't get off the ground.

One potential line of criticism is that any theory which attempts to address the problem of other minds must at least do justice to the, surely intuitively correct, idea that there is the possibility that when I have a conversation with other people, that they're not people like me, they could be automata or something like that. Does your

argument accept the admissibility of that sceptical doubt or does it deny it?

In terms of admissibility, I'd want to say that the way language works makes its threat a kind of inevitability. The threat of scepticism is never finally removed in the kind of account I give, but not because the authenticity or sincerity of an expression is something hidden or unpresentable. Rather, it is because it's part of the structure of any iterable trait that it is always possible to repeat and hence mimic it, act it, stage-play it. This is a structural possibility of all uses of signs. We could call that the truth of scepticism. So I don't think that anything I've said would make scepticism seem utterly idle. We can now see what spurs it on, and will always do so.

Do you anticipate more philosophy being done in the future which refuses to see itself in terms of the categories of analytic and continental philosophy, or do you think that the old divisions will endure?

There are, in fact, a growing number of people who do philosophy in ways which deliberately resist being captured by that distinction. That's a tiny minority, but I also think that it's a growing minority, and the reason why I think it is growing is that it's becoming increasingly clear that the analytic/continental distinction doesn't cut things up in ways which are philosophically significant. Changes within the analytic movement are relevant here. In its early phases, analytic philosophy was typically defined in terms of conceptual analysis, where conceptual analysis was thought of as an activity wholly distinct from scientific, empirical enquiry. In more recent times, that view of analytic philosophy has been challenged and rejected by more and more people, particularly in America. Perhaps the dominant kind of analytic philosophy today, at least in America, although it's growing here too, is philosophical naturalism. This is the tradition of philosophy opposed to the one I see myself located in, the post-Kantian tradition which doesn't see that kind of continuity between philosophy and science. For me, and I think for many others, this is where the most fundamental issues and disputes lie today. And this is why concern with the demarcation of analytic philosophy from continental philosophy is becoming less and less significant and is being abandoned by more and more people within the profession. In that respect, even though the number of people working between the traditions is a tiny minority, the functioning of the distinction is less and less pertinent.

Could I just ask briefly how you will be continuing your research in the near future?

On Being with Others takes its point of departure from a problem in epistemology, the problem of other minds. But it broaches at a number of points, and yet does not investigate at all, questions which more traditionally belong to ethics. And the relation to an other is clearly not only an epistemological issue, it's always also an ethical matter. So I have hopes of producing a kind of *On Being with Others 2* (or too) which will take its point of departure not from epistemology but ethics. In a rather crude way you could call that ethics after Levinas (although my own work is not at this time heavily influenced by Levinas), because Levinas was a philosopher who insisted on seeing ethics in terms of the relation to the other, and the appearance of the other as being an irreducibly ethical relation.

Select Bibliography

'Communication and writing: a public language argument', *Proceedings of the Aristotelian Society*, 100, May 2000

Arguing with Derrida (editor), *Ratio*, Special Issue, 13: 4, Blackwell, 2000

The Edinburgh Encyclopedia of Continental Philosophy (general editor), Edinburgh University Press, 1999

'The ethics of exclusion', in *Questioning Ethics*, edited by R. Kearney and M. Dooley, Routledge, 1999

On Being With Others: Heidegger–Wittgenstein–Derrida, Routledge, 1998

13 Sartre's Existentialism

In conversation with Christina Howells

If you asked a number of Anglo-American philosophers to give a brief description of Sartre's existential philosophy, it is likely that many of them would mention the primacy of individual existence, human freedom, a lack of objective values, and, half-seriously, Parisian café life. You would probably get a version of existentialism as a kind of humanism, with the emphasis placed on the necessity for individuals to make their own way in the world.

Certainly, there is more than an element of truth in this conception of Sartrean existentialism. Sartre did think that we are condemned to be free – that there is an absolute requirement to choose the kind of life that we lead, the morals that we espouse, even the emotions that we manifest. However, the truth about Sartre's philosophy is more strange than might at first be supposed.

The strangeness of his philosophy derives in part from the way that he conceptualises consciousness and the human subject. In *Being and Nothingness*, Sartre's major existential work, he argues that being for-itself (*pour-soi*) or consciousness is defined by its *nothingness*. It stands in a peculiar relation of *nihilation* to the rest of being (being in-itself or *en-soi*). He means by this that the for-itself is always aware that it is *not* the multitude of objects towards which it is directed. It is in this awareness that the freedom of the for-itself is manifest.

Of particular significance is the fact that the for-itself can adopt any number of attitudes, including denial, towards the objects to which it is directed. This detachment from the given order of things means that there is the permanent possibility that things might be other than they are. So freedom is rooted in a detachment that is a consequence of the fact that the for-itself is essentially a nothingness.

However, the fact that the for-itself is always and inevitably free does not mean that people make their choices in a vacuum. Rather, they are confronted by the *facticity* of their particular lives. Facticity includes all the things about an individual that cannot be changed at any given point in time – for example, their sex, age, social class and, in Sartre's later work, even genetic and psychological dispositions. Choices then are made against this kind of background – and consequently, the Sartrean conception of freedom is less radical than many have supposed.

The role of the self, and its relation to human freedom, is also significant in this schema. Sartre denied that individuals have essential selves. Rather, he claimed that the self is a construct – an object of consciousness – that is built out of past experiences and behaviour. As such, in principle, the self is something that is both chosen and that can be changed. However, in practice, it is not easy to choose a course of action that is out of character with the constituted self. Consequently, the self imposes another limit on human freedom.

The two ideas discussed above – that the Sartrean conception of the for-itself places the human subject (but not, in the same way, the Self) radically in question, and that Sartrean freedom is not as unconditional as might be supposed – are both prominent in Christina Howells's work. Significantly, in her recent book, *Derrida: Deconstruction from Phenomenology to Ethics*, she points to some interesting correspondences between the ways in which Sartre, on the one hand, and

Derrida, on the other, have treated consciousness and the human subject. According to Howells, these correspondences are not coincidental, but rather they are indicative of the enduring influence and significance of Sartre's thought, even for a thinker who certainly at one time saw himself as intractably opposed to Sartre's ideas.

It is striking that many of the philosophers we've interviewed for this book have not come to philosophy by a direct path. I believe that's also the case with you?
Indeed, I read French and English at university. And then my Ph.D. was on Sartre's theory of literature. At that point, I almost moved into the philosophy department, because my supervisor believed that I should. But in the end we agreed that I was doing theory of literature, and that I should stay in the French department.

At this time did you attend any lectures on Sartre given by philosophers?
No, at that stage I didn't. I went to hear Richard Wollheim talking about aesthetics, and other philosophers on all kinds of topics, but not Sartre. In fact, at this time, philosophers weren't greatly interested in French existentialist thought, and that's one of the reasons that I didn't want to move into a philosophy department. I thought that even if the subject matter lent itself better to philosophy, there wasn't anyone that I wanted to supervise me.

It is probably fair to say that in this country Sartre is known primarily as one of the leading figures of the existentialist movement. What do you take existentialism to be? And what is it that makes Sartre an existentialist?

I take existentialism to be the focus on the freedom and self-making of the human being, and his or her insertion into the world. A focus on these things, rather than on questions of logic, or truth, or any kind of essentialist or empirical psychology. And Sartre really is the prime exponent of existentialism, these are his interests. I can't quite see how else it would be possible to classify him.

Is existentialism, defined in this fairly broad way, something that comes into being with say Kierkegaard, or is existentialism just a label that has been applied retrospectively to these older thinkers?

That's an interesting question. I don't really know. I know that historically it is supposed to have originated with Kierkegaard and then moved on, but this always seems to me to be a rather odd idea. I mean you could say that Pascal or Montaigne were existentialist thinkers, and you could probably go even further back. I suppose it is the twentieth century conceptualisation of existentialism, and then the incorporation of Kierkegaard, that has led to people being collected under the name. But there is no reason to be nominalist about it, it's fine to have the term and collect people up with similar attitudes.

What about the technical definition of existentialism, that existence precedes essence? Is this redundant? Or just not very useful?

Well, I was avoiding it, because it seems to me that without explanation it is very hard to see what on earth it means, but in so far as it means that we do not have a pre-existing self, which organises our behaviour, but rather that we create our self as we go along, through our existence and activities, I think this would be a reasonable way of beginning to understand existentialism.

In *Being and Nothingness,* Sartre's major existentialist work, *he* divides being into two major realms, *being in itself (en-soi)* and *being for itself (pour-soi).* What does he see as constituting each realm?

What's often said about *Being and Nothingness* is that it contains six pages on being and 660 pages on nothingness! However, in terms of the *pour-soi* and the *en-soi*, Sartre says that the *pour-soi* is human consciousness – though they're not completely identical – and the *en-soi* is the rest. And the rest then is not only material objects, but also our nature, our past and the body.

Where do the terms *en-soi* and *pour-soi* come from? There is this notion, in Sartre, that consciousness is reflexive, that is, that consciousness is always, inevitably aware of itself. Am I right in thinking that the term *pour-soi* – or being for-itself – is supposed to imply this reflexivity of consciousness?

Yes. Well, it's partly historical, since he is using pre-existing terms. Probably the apparent split in the *en-soi* is a little bit misleading, but in the *pour-soi* it is vital, and it is part of the meaning of the term. In other words, it *is* the reflexivity of consciousness which is the *pour-soi*, and from whence the human subject arises. Sartre calls this the circuit of selfhood.

How does the classical Sartrean idea that we are condemned to be free fit in with this notion of the *pour-soi*? In other words, how does the fact that we are beings for ourselves lead to the idea of absolute freedom?

I think it is best to think of this negatively, so that we are condemned to be free precisely because we can't become *en-soi*. We have to stay as consciousnesses. Consciousness works through negation and nihilation

in Sartre's account. When consciousness intends the world in the phenomenological sense, it simultaneously nihilates it – that is, it knows
that it is not that which it is conscious of. Consciousness therefore can't
achieve the self-coincidence that the *en-soi* has precisely by its nature.
It's part of the rhetoric and metaphorical side of *Being and Nothingness*
that we are condemned to be free, and we're condemned to be free in
so far as consciousness has no possibility of achieving any kind of
self-coincidence except by coming to an end in death.

So this notion of freedom is far removed from a common-sense notion of free choice?

Absolutely. In fact, I can never quite understand where the idea comes
from that Sartre believes we are free to do anything we please. He
certainly doesn't say it in *Being and Nothingness*. He concentrates
there on the difficulty in changing, on the difficulty in doing anything
other than following the path that we are already following. This
difficulty has to do situation and facticity – where facticity refers to
those things about ourselves that we cannot change – which are
inescapable.

The notion that Sartre holds on to from the start, right through to
his death, is the notion of the freedom of consciousness. But how that
works out in practice develops considerably, so that in the later Sartre,
the room for free activity is much smaller and the importance of facticity and situation is much greater. And indeed facticity – for example, in
Being and Nothingness, our age, our class origin, our sex, and so on –
has, by the time he writes on Flaubert, come to include all sorts of
psychological and family structures, which restrict practical freedom,
but which don't undermine the idea that we're free through
consciousness.

Sartre contends that we are forever trying to escape that anguish which is resultant of our freedom. Why do we find freedom so difficult?

I suppose our freedom is difficult because it is so radical and it goes so deep. I think if it was freedom of behaviour or freedom of activity, it wouldn't necessarily be particularly difficult to face up to. But because it is also freedom to choose not only what kind of life we are going to lead, but also what kind of person we are going to be, what kinds of ethics we are going to adopt, and indeed, what kinds of emotions we are going to manifest, this radical kind of freedom offers choice on a level that as human beings we're not really comfortable with.

What kinds of strategies does he envisage that we employ in order to escape freedom?

Well, he's got two terms, the coward and the bastard. The coward, I think, is the character who accepts ready-made values through the state, or the church or politics. The bastard is the one who wants to impose his choices on other people. They are both evasive strategies, according to Sartre, because they both refuse to acknowledge that each individual is making a choice for him or herself.

Sartre gives quite long explanations of the different ways we may evade responsibility for ourselves. We might turn to psychoanalysis, for example, to say that we have been made the way that we are by our parents, or to Marxism, to say that we have been determined by history and politics.

And the idea is that despite adopting these strategies, ultimately we can't escape a recognition of our own freedom?

We can hide it quite well from ourselves, I think. This question of how much Sartre thinks we're conscious of is interesting, partly because of his rejection of much of Freud, and particularly his rejection of the conscious/unconscious distinction. However, it would be quite wrong to think that Sartre believes that everything is conscious, because he discusses the pre-conscious. What he dislikes in Freud is the idea that there is an unconscious realm, which is barred off from consciousness. If you look at his existential/psychoanalytical studies – mainly of Baudelaire and Flaubert – he talks there about the different levels of consciousness, right down to a level which is deeply masked from oneself.

It's interesting that Sartre makes some fairly radical claims about the nature of freedom. In his early work on the emotions, he explicitly argues that one chooses one's emotions as a way to transform the world. And in *Being and Nothingness*, he gives the example of the person who is depressed or sad, who greets a friend in the street, and Sartre asks what happens to the person's sadness during the course of the meeting, and he answers that it has been cast off to be reclaimed later on. This idea that we can choose our emotions suggests a very radical conception of freedom. Is this Sartre's view, and is it sustainable?

This is a very interesting issue. The theory of emotions is one of the theories that I most enjoy in Sartre, because it is so provocative and people often object to it strongly. But it's important to note that he distinguishes between states and feelings and emotions. So one can't actually slip between the terms depression, unhappiness and sadness, and so on, as if they were identical.

The *Sketch of a Theory of Emotion* is about emotion, and Sartre says in it that he is not talking about states, so he will be describing the moment of happy surprise, rather than a period of contentment, and he gives the example of someone getting a prize or a present, and reacting very exuberantly, whereas, of course, they could have chosen with the same amount of surprise, and equally genuinely, to react in a more controlled way.

Taking the example of putting aside one's sadness to greet a friend in the street, that seems to me to be a very good example, because people do it all the time. For example, if they have split up with their girlfriend, and they meet someone on the street, they don't want to talk about that, so for the time being they put it aside, and they talk about something else. And they are sometimes surprised to find afterwards that it has slipped their mind momentarily, the dreadful thing, while they were talking.

Just going back to this notion that there are states, rather than emotions, that perhaps it isn't possible simply to cast aside. I'm thinking here about clinical depression. If one wanted to develop a critique of Sartre, it might be possible to throw up his idea that there is no human essence against the seeming fact that one can be infected in a profound way by a state like depression. Surely this shouldn't be allowed in, in the Sartrean schema?

There are two ways of answering that. One is to say that this is something that Sartre and Simone de Beauvoir disagreed about very much in the early years. You find in their exchange of letters, quite interestingly, de Beauvoir insisting that she is not free to get over feelings of jealousy, or hurt that men have caused her, and Sartre insisting that she is, and there's quite a strong disagreement over this. I think, if I'm understanding you correctly, that you might have more sympathy with de Beauvoir than Sartre.

But also it has to be said that the later Sartre seems to have really rather a different position, a much more subtle position. Probably the best place to look at this is in his account of Flaubert's fall, which was deemed to have been an epileptic fit, which he had when he was out in a carriage, after which he had to stay home – he couldn't leave to train to become a lawyer, as he had planned to do – and he became a writer. Sartre points out that certain theories of epilepsy claim that it has an hysterical origin, and he discusses the idea that we can benefit from illness, that it is both something that we undergo and also an active strategy. Again he has a quite explicit conception of different levels of consciousness, and he lists about nine levels at which it is possible to say that Flaubert's fall is intentional. Not deliberated and chosen, but nevertheless intentional.

Another criticism of Sartre that is sometimes made is that his notion of freedom suggests chaos, inconsistency, anarchy, randomness and so on in the choices that people make day to day. The typical response to this kind of criticism is to point to Sartre's notion of a 'fundamental project'. What does he mean by this, and how is it possible to reconcile it with his idea of absolute freedom, and more specifically, the idea that consciousness is always separated from its past?

Well, to put it very simply, for Sartre I am completely free, starting from where I am. Starting from where I am means both my situation and my facticity, including my past. He says, in *Being and Nothingness*, I can change, but it's not particularly easy. It is certainly not as easy as people thinking about Sartre imagine that he believes it to be. This is partly because of a view I think he shares with Freud, about the person being a totality rather than a collection. We can't really change piecemeal. If we want to change one bit of ourselves, it involves a structural change – though he doesn't use that terminology – if you change one thing, then everything changes. It's all part of a significant whole, and it can't just be tinkered with.

An example in *Being and Nothingness* that I like, because I feel that it illustrates very well what he means by this, is that of a hike that some friends take together. They go on a long walk, and one of them says he is too tired and he has to stop. And Sartre asks, what does it mean that he is too tired? Assuming that he is just tired like everybody else, why does he decide that he is going to give up, and could he in fact have continued? Sartre says, well, he could have acted differently, of course, but at what price? And he says that the price would have been a reconfiguring of the fundamental project. So if his fundamental project, of which he is not explicitly conscious, involves, as priorities, self-preservation and his comfort, and if these are more important than duty to friends, conviviality, and so on, these would then be radically altered if he, in the situation described, completed the last few miles, and walked to the finish of the hike. Sartre argues that this isn't easy to do, people just can't change piecemeal.

One of the worries that people have about Sartrean existentialism is that the idea of the *pour-soi* (consciousness) effectively does away with the human subject. In fact, I think I'm right in saying that in *The Transcendence of the Ego,* he precisely argues that the ego is not the essential self. Do you think it is possible to talk of the human subject, and if so, how does it fit into Sartre's philosophy?

In *The Transcendence of the Ego*, Sartre does reject the transcendental ego. He says that the ego is transcendent, not transcendental. That is to say, he argues that the ego is created, not immanent. But although he doesn't talk about the human subject, what he does say is by no means incompatible with the subject. He is talking about the ego, but the ego isn't the subject, the subject results from the kinds of reflexivity we talked about earlier. The reflexivity of consciousness, the circuit of selfness.

The idea of the subject is complex in Sartre, and it is one of the most interesting to work on, because the vocabulary that he uses to talk about it in *Being and Nothingness* is really very close to the vocabulary of various post-structuralists. So he talks about it being deferred, about it being dispersed, he says that the subject is diasporic, that it constantly escapes itself, and so on. And this is why *Existentialism as a Humanism* is such an unfortunate title, because it pushes people to look for a different kind of subject in *Being and Nothingness* from what they are going to find.

Following on from this, it is striking that in your book on Derrida, you point to some interesting correspondences between the Derridian idea of de-centring and Sartre's theory of consciousness. What do you take these correspondences to be and how significant do you think Sartre's influence on Derrida is?

I do think that the Sartrean notion of the subject and Derridian *différance* are closely related, though I don't think that this is necessarily where Sartre has been most influential on Derrida. In fact, it seems to me that Derrida is influenced by Sartre at lots of different stages in his writing. One of the best examples is in his work on Husserl. There is a section in *Being and Nothingness*, where Sartre, in modern terms, deconstructs Husserl's conception of consciousness. And then you have Derrida's *Voice and Phenomenon* in 1966, where in more detail, Derrida carries out a very similar analysis, at greater length, but with no reference to Sartre.

I've talked with Derrida about this, and I think that his present position is somewhat different from his earlier rejection of Sartre. In the mid-1960s, he was very hard on Sartre, but in contrast to that early position you've now got the essay he wrote for *Les Temps Modernes'* fiftieth anniversary issue, where he talks about how important Sartre was to him when he was an adolescent, and he also says that he had a strange amnesia about Sartre, that he forgot that he knew about Sartre. He had to reread Sartre to write the essay for *Les Temps Modernes*, and he kept finding in Sartre all these notions that he enormously liked, that he had used himself, and that he had forgotten were present in Sartre. In 1999, Derrida came to the Sartre group conference in Paris – there was a whole day on Sartre and Derrida – and he was very open to the idea that he had refused a heritage when he was younger, because it was something against which he was defining himself.

You mention in your book, on a number of different occasions, how difficult it is to read Derrida. It is also the case that Sartre can be very difficult. What motivates this continental style, if you'll excuse the geographical oversimplification?

I don't think Sartre is ever deliberately difficult. He wrote very fast, he took drugs so that he could write more quickly, and he didn't self-correct.

Derrida is a different kettle of fish. Like Sartre, he has a paradoxical way of thinking, but I don't think it is that which is difficult in Derrida. I think it is rather his use of language, because he wants to use language to make it say things that it hasn't previously said. And he has got different devices for doing this. I remember an argument he had with Habermas about whether or not he conflates philosophy and literature, and he denies that he does. But that doesn't mean that some of the features of a literary style don't appear in his work. He does use the materiality of language, its allusiveness and wordplay in order to bring out connections; intertextual references that aren't explicit; allusions that aren't explicit; neologisms; and what he calls paleonomy, where he takes an old word, and puts a new concept in it. All this for Derrida, I think, is to try to force us to think. He says at one point, we haven't even begun to think.

I've heard him defend the difficulty of his work in a conference, and the defence was along the lines that it was a specific type of philosophy, and it was technical, and there was no reason why anyone reading it should immediately understand it, anymore than they would any other specialised, technical language.

Is it worth the effort then on the part of analytic philosophers, given the kinds of things they tend to be interested in, to attempt to get to grips with Derrida?

Well, as I'm not an analytic philosopher, I don't really know. I would have thought it would be, because I know how much there is in Derrida, and therefore I would think it worthwhile for anybody to make the effort. I'm not sure though that I'm very keen on the idea of transforming Derrida into terms that analytic philosophy can cope with and use. I think that you'd lose much of the specificity that way, and you could well be left with banality.

What about Sartre? You're not keen that analytic philosophers should adopt a pick and mix approach with Derrida, using the bits they find useful and discarding the rest. Do you feel the same way about Sartre's work? There have been attempts by analytic philosophers to show how Sartre might be helpful.

Well, analytic philosophers have written on Sartre. But again there is the risk of transforming the philosophers into something they're not, and making them say something they weren't saying. For example, bad faith and self-deception – obviously there are very interesting connections. In what way is bad faith a form of self-deception? Bad faith and self-deception seem fairly similar, yet different in ways worth thinking about. But when you extract from a long elaborated discussion a kernel which is then acceptable to analytic philosophy, whether it is about *being with others*, or about what Derrida might mean by *différance*, if he were prepared to express it quite differently, you've lost too much.

So I'm not against pick-and-mix, I think pick-and-mix is fine, it's the transforming into something quite different that seems to me rather unfortunate. I'm all in favour of dialogue, but people need to look at these philosophers more on their own terms.

Some people talk about there being a crisis in analytic philosophy. Is there a sense in which there is a comparable crisis in the kind of tradition that Sartre and Derrida inhabit? I'm thinking here of problems of the grounding of ethics, the desire in French philosophy for the human subject to be reclaimed, and the debate about Heidegger's relationship to the Nazis.

My view of this is that the heart of the matter is keeping various different levels separate. You need to separate the metaphysical (and anti-metaphysical) from the other side, which is the ethical and political, rather than trying to assimilate them. You have to distinguish between ontology and praxis and not to try to assimilate them. So, for example, it is not very useful for the purposes of ethics and politics, where agency is vital, to have the metaphysical (or anti-metaphysical) conclusion that the human subject is radically in question, so you separate the domains.

In fact, this is one of the problems that I have been looking at recently in feminist philosophy. You'll find that feminist theory, in its desire to side with that tradition in continental philosophy that wishes to place the human subject in question, has become fascinated with the possibility of getting rid of the femaleness in the feminine, the grounded nature of the subject, and so on. But obviously these are possibilities that quite likely run counter to its ethical and political aims.

So the solution to the problem of the subject and its relation to ethics lies in separating out the two fields? So you do your metaphysics (or your anti-metaphysics), but you bracket this out when you're doing your politics?

Well, this is a version of Derrida's solution. When I heard him suggest it, I was vastly relieved. He stated that deconstruction would never stop him crying out *vive la revolution* at the appropriate moment! But in more theoretical terms, deconstruction can help us precisely to rethink the relationship between subjectivity and ethics, law and justice, ethics and politics.

To finish, is it possible to say anything broad about the value of the kinds of philosophy that Derrida and Sartre represent?

I think that it forces us to think against ourselves. Both Sartre and Derrida say this about themselves, that they have always thought against their earlier views. Sartre says that he has always been a traitor, he doesn't mean against his friends, but against his own work, and for this reason he feels that his previous work and ideas are part of the past and gone, and that he is going to move on.

And certainly, although Derrida doesn't quite say this, he too is not at all afraid to move against his earlier thinking. I suppose one argues that it fits in with his idea of the deconstruction of the notion of authorship, that one doesn't have to homogenise and totalise his works.

Select Bibliography

French Women Philosophers. Subjectivity, Identity and Alterity. A Contemporary Reader, Routledge, forthcoming 2003

Derrida: Deconstruction from Phenomenology to Ethics, Polity, 1999

The Cambridge Companion to Sartre (editor), Cambridge, 1992

Sartre: The Necessity of Freedom, Cambridge, 1988

Sartre's Theory of Literature, MRHA, 1979

14   Post-Analytic Philosophy

In conversation with Stephen Mulhall

Does philosophy make progress? It certainly progresses, in the sense that things change, agendas move on and debates are taken further or abandoned. Philosophy is not static, although it differs from science, in the sense that the philosophy of centuries ago is still considered valuable to philosophers working today, whereas the science of centuries past belongs only to history.

Perhaps because of this, philosophy's relation to its past is problematic. On the one hand, it does not want to become trapped in its past, still regurgitating tired scholastic arguments from the Middle Ages. On the other hand, the past cannot simply be sloughed off, since the insights and arguments of the great figures of the past continue to speak to us and inform the subject.

This problem is central to the project of post-analytic philosophy. Analytic philosophy is a term which is used with varying degrees of precision. Most generally, it is used to refer to the whole tradition of twentieth-century Anglo-American philosophy. But aside from this purely historical–geographical usage, there is a more precise meaning which tries to describe a type and style of philosophy which is seen as: rooted in logical argument; having the philosophy of language and meaning as its primary subject matter; striving for rigour; and taking as its model scientific enquiry rather than literary or artistic expression.

The idea of a post-analytic philosophy is taken up by Stephen Mulhall in this interview. Mulhall has been described as the archetypal post-analytic philosopher. But what does such an epithet mean? It certainly does not mean that Mulhall rejects in its entirety the conception of philosophy set out above. Post-analytic philosophy is not about making a clean break from philosophy's recent – or distant – past, but about moving forwards while retaining what is of value from the past.

Of course, there is a sense in which all good philosophy tries to do this. But sometimes, in order to really move on, a clearer break with the past is required. The Italian philosopher Michele Marsonet has used the key thesis of Thomas Kuhn's great work, *The Structure of Scientific Revolutions*, to illustrate this.

Kuhn argued that scientists in any given epoch tend to work within what he called a 'paradigm'. This is like a set of basic principles and assumptions which provides the framework within which all scientific work takes place. For a while, science proceeds quite happily within a paradigm. But after a while, the paradigm itself begins to fracture. Flaws in the framework come to light and eventually, the paradigm becomes unsustainable. An intellectual revolution takes place and a new paradigm establishes itself. In time, this paradigm is itself accepted and scientists carry on their work within the framework it provides.

This peaceful period where scientists work happily within the paradigm is termed 'normal science'. However, it should not be thought that those working within the paradigm are necessarily aware that they are merely working within one paradigm in a sequence of many. Scientists come to take the framework for granted, partly because a paradigm is essential in order for any normal scientific research to be done. In these circumstances, one can mistake the settled status quo for the one true way to do science.

Whether or not Kuhn accurately describes the progress of science, the developments he describes could certainly also occur in philosophy. It could be that a way of doing philosophy establishes itself, and that the community of philosophers happily work within it, forgetting that they are merely working within one paradigm, a paradigm which is itself historically and culturally specific, and one which will, in time, reveal its own fractures.

Is analytic philosophy one such paradigm? Even if it is not quite a paradigm in the strict Kuhnian sense, could it be that Anglo-American philosophy has settled too easily into a way of doing philosophy which cannot endure? If so, then one must consider what happens when the next intellectual revolution comes. What will the new philosophical paradigm look like? Can we move on to a philosophy without a paradigm, or must a new paradigm be established? Would such a new paradigm be a complete break with the past or will it bring some of the best of the past with it?

Stephen Mulhall's philosophy deals with such issues, though not, it must be stressed, within a specifically Kuhnian framework. How does philosophy move on and what is its relation to its past? These are questions of the utmost personal and professional concern to Mulhall.

One of your greatest influences, Stanley Cavell, talked about his philosophical mind being split. When you think about how you came to philosophy, is there anything in the way your mind was that led you to philosophy or was it accidental?

The kind of interests I had which made me think I ought to do philosophy at university depended as much on a sense of the connection between philosophy and science as anything, paradoxically. It was things like those Raymond Burke programmes about perception, and particularly the science of perception, which is, of course, exactly the angle or aspect of philosophy I'm much less interested in now.

When Balliol College at Oxford gave me a reading list of texts to look at before I came up for the first year to read Philosophy, Politics and Economics, one of those was A. J. Ayer's *Language, Truth and Logic*. I just found that a completely traumatic experience, because in effect, by the end of chapter four, all of the things that mattered to me about philosophy – ethics, aesthetics, religion – he had effectively dismissed as completely meaningless and no part of any serious philosophical project. I believed him. I took it that this book had been set for me, not as a kind of reference point against which I could react critically, but as a sample of what it was to do philosophy.

So when I arrived at Balliol the first thing I did was have an interview with the master, Anthony Kenny, and I told him that if this was philosophy, I didn't want anything to do with it, and that I'd much rather do English. In fact, I had an interview with one of the English tutors there, but he was so resistant to the idea of taking anyone extra on that in the end I didn't do it, thankfully.

I think that the way in which I reacted to Ayer, as well as the fact that it was Ayer I was reacting to, was at the root of something for me. What I really disliked about the analytical philosophy I came across is epitomised in Ayer – that sense of taking empirical discourse, and scientific discourse in particular, as paradigmatic of meaningful discourse more generally; and the sense that realms of value, aspects of significance to human life that depend on something more than the perfectly interesting project of discovering the truth about nature, should be regarded not just as uninteresting or a ghetto of philosophy, but as essentially meaningless. That is still the aspect of analytical philosophy I find difficult to handle.

Of course, the direction I went in response to that is the direction I still find interesting, namely, a sense that there's some kind of open border between philosophy and literature.

It's interesting that the question of the possibility of doing philosophy is one which has weighed upon your mind. You read Ayer and wondered how we could do philosophy after this, and you had a similar experience later with Wittgenstein.

What happened, in effect, was that around the middle of the second year, I did the late Wittgenstein paper. That really completely knocked me off my horse. I had got on top of some of the basics in analytic philosophy as Oxford presents them to you. However, I was feeling a bit dissatisfied, probably coming back to the initial response I had to Ayer, but this time it was more to do with the kinds of issues people like Quine and Davidson took to be definitive of what philosophy should be doing. What Wittgenstein did was to provide a kind of sustained elaboration of those sorts of anxieties and worries about the way analytical philosophy thinks of itself, but also a way out of it. Having Peter Hacker as your tutor on Wittgenstein, as I did, means what you get is an incredibly rigorous argument against analytical philosophy, or at least the aspects of analytical philosophy that Wittgenstein found troubling. You don't simply get Wittgenstein presented to you as someone who has a completely different way of looking at things. What you get is a sense of Wittgenstein who moves from a position of centrally inhabiting the tradition, to a position of very radical criticism of it, but someone who as a result of that process is extremely well versed in the tradition he's criticising and incapable of entirely leaving it behind. What he's going to count as philosophy has to bear some kind of relationship to the analytical figures he was educated by – Frege and Russell particularly. You can't understand what he wants to do with philosophy except by going through those paradigms.

What was it about Wittgenstein which gave you the worry that, after him, there's nowhere to go with philosophy?

I was perfectly happy to spend a lot of time working out just exactly how, at the level of finer detail, Wittgenstein's critiques of analytical philosophy might be made good. But you can only do that for so long. If you're personally convinced that at least in the broad brush these criticisms Wittgenstein makes do work, it can become extremely tedious to keep on doing it, particularly when it meets such unremitting resistance. I couldn't imagine myself spending twenty or thirty years as a professional academic doing nothing but that.

The question then becomes, what do you do with your own relation to Wittgenstein, if you really do take him to have made some kind of definitive step beyond the way that tradition thinks of itself?

My concern was that it is very difficult to see how to go on with and from Wittgenstein without your own voice being completely submerged. You either find yourself doing no more than reiterating what he's already done, or you find an aspect or an area of analytical philosophy which Wittgenstein didn't explicitly talk about and you see what you can do with his methods there. That holds certain attractions, I think, but it also holds great risks of just being very mechanical in what you're doing. A third way is acknowledging what Wittgenstein has done, and remaining indebted to that, but doing something that much more intimately expresses your own interests in the subject. That was the difficulty I found, trying to imagine what that would look like.

It was Cavell who helped you out of this cul-de-sac. How did that happen?

While studying for my MA in Toronto, I visited a friend of mine, Adan Swift, at Harvard. He knew I was interested in Wittgenstein and he presented me with a copy of Cavell's *The Claim of Reason*, which was the first time I'd come across it. That was the point at which Cavell appeared in my intellectual life. It seemed to me clear from the *Claim of Reason* that Cavell had a very individual story to tell about Wittgenstein's relation to analytical philosophy.

What Cavell was doing with Wittgenstein just looked radically different from what I'd seen anybody else do with him. I suppose the most obvious indicator of that is Cavell's style. Cavell writes philosophy in an extremely unorthodox, idiosyncratic way. That was really the first example I came across of a Wittgensteinian who took the question of inheriting Wittgenstein to be a question as much about his style as about what he had to say. Although there were many, many strengths in the way people like Baker and Hacker read and made use of Wittgenstein's text, that sense of Wittgenstein's voice can be lost in the way they utilise the *Investigations*, and other texts, to do what they want to do with it.

For me, Cavell was the only person I'd come across who, whatever you want to say about his text, doesn't lose that sense of Wittgenstein's voice. One can see how the way he writes philosophy is an inflection of the way in which Wittgenstein writes philosophy. That was what was liberating for me. It meant that what it might mean to do philosophy in a Wittgensteinian way suddenly had an alternative paradigm. As well as presenting an alternative way of reading and understanding Wittgenstein, it was also clear that what Cavell was doing with Wittgenstein was not something Wittgenstein would have done. Cavell's own voice is as evident in his writing, as Wittgenstein's voice is too.

It showed you the possibility of continuing an authentically Wittgensteinian style of philosophy, but in your own voice.
Exactly. It was not some kind of ventriloquising. There were people in the first and second generation of Wittgensteinian philosophers who

did have an unusual or distinctive style to what they did, but it often seemed to teeter on the edge of parody of Wittgenstein's own style. That was obviously something which was made much of by analytical critics of their work. Whereas Cavell, it seems to me, is not in that sense a replica. That made me think that you didn't have to suppress your own individuality entirely, in order to do what Wittgenstein wanted to do. That mattered a lot.

Your philosophical development has cut across the traditional analytic/continental divide. Do you think there just isn't anything to this split at all, or do you think that it is something less than has been supposed?

It's certainly the case that there's something to it. Someone trained exclusively in analytical philosophy would be, I think, more or less bereft if parachuted into the way in which late twentieth century French and German philosophy gets conducted. But one of the things which seems to me obviously not true is that there is *a* split. One of the very unfortunate ways of picturing this whole problem is to think of it as involving, on the one hand, the tradition of analytical philosophy and, on the other hand, the continental tradition. What's plain, if you look at the history of European receptions of Kant, is that you have a number of different traditions. You have the tradition that goes into German idealism; you have various critics of that, like Marx; then you have people like Nietzsche and Schopenhauer in the late nineteenth century; then again you have Husserl and the origins of phenomenology as a tradition, with Heidegger coming into that story and Sartre taking it up in a certain way; and you have the post-structuralists, the people interested in deconstruction. It's a very complicated story. If you look at the multiplicity, it allows far more differentiations than you might think, but there's a kind of genealogy, a historical narrative that holds them together – a certain kind of inheritance of problems and questions. Even when radical methodological changes are introduced, they are introduced in response to the history of the subject as they understand it.

In a certain sense, that's also true of analytical philosophy. In one way, what one might call pure analytical philosophy is already over. If you think of it as starting with Frege and going through Russell, the *Tractatus* and logical positivism, by the time you get to the 1950s, you're already going to have a certain amount of difficulty identifying a simple story of reproduction. People like Quine and Davidson can and have been presented as radical internal critics of analytical philosophy. Much of what's done in the philosophy of mind and the philosophy of language now after Quine and Davidson is itself more or less radical in its alterations to their own assumptions. Then you've got the people I've spent a lot of time working on in the area of philosophy of language, ethics and political philosophy, people like Taylor, Murdoch, Nussbaum and Diamond. These are people who also have a very troubled relation to the pure tradition of analytical philosophy. So again, precisely because of the multiplicity of differences, I have much less sense of a great abyss between any two of them. The room for dialogue seems to me to be quite extensive.

To keep philosophy going and to keep it alive, given these various inheritances, there's one particular challenge you identify, which is modernism. Taking this from your introduction to Stanley Cavell, you say, of modernism in art, 'Modernism thus appears as a condition in which serious painters are no longer able to rely upon agreed conventions inherited from their tradition to establish that what they do is indeed painting'. Can we translate this directly to philosophy and say: Modernism thus appears as a condition in

which serious philosophers are no longer able to rely upon agreed conventions inherited from their tradition to establish that what they do is indeed philosophy?

All analogies are going to limp at some point, but I think this one actually has legs to it. It seems to me to be a very accurate characterisation of Wittgenstein's relation to the analytical tradition that it's an undismissible problem in the history of the subject for him, even though his work isn't replete with historical references. It's plain that he could only understand what he was doing as standing in some kind of relation to what Frege, Russell and the *Tractatus* were attempting to do.

I think this is an accurate characterisation of much of what gets called post-analytic philosophy. I think people like Taylor, MacIntyre, Cavell and Nussbaum are people who have clearly been trained in the analytical tradition, who are perfectly competent in its techniques and approaches, but who think that there's something which has gone radically wrong with it, some sense that it's reached a certain kind of impoverishment, that for various reasons, both internal and external – reasons that in some cases are still very puzzling for them – it's lost touch in a certain kind of way with what really brings us to philosophy in the first place. Not that it's entirely dissociated from those original motivations, but that it has developed in various ways and begun to think in various ways that unduly limit our sense of what resources we might have to bring to bear in philosophy and what might count as doing philosophy. So they do subject it to quite a radical critique. But in all of those cases, I think, they would regard what they are doing as, in a certain sense, an extension of that tradition, they're not losing faith with it altogether. What they see themselves as doing is trying to return it to its best self, the kinds of aspects of it which they took to be most compelling in the first place through their education in the subject and their initial attraction to it.

To sum up, perhaps post-analytic philosophy can be characterised in this way: it is a style of philosophy that meets the challenge of modernity by engaging with its past in such a way that, neither dismissing it nor moving on from it uncritically, it remains recognisably the same subject.

That way of putting it raises one of the problems with the idea of a modernist relation to any given tradition or discipline, because it looks as if it ought to be one of the commitments or obligations of *any* philosopher to question or critically relate to their own assumptions about method. After all, it's a perfectly standard way of introducing the notion of philosophy to say that in any disciplinary area – history, art, science, ethics – there are a certain number of things that inevitably have to be taken for granted. Because they are founding assumptions, their discipline and the disciplinary tools they have at their disposal are not going to be capable of properly evaluating those assumptions, since all of these tools precisely rest on taking those assumptions for granted. So the philosopher comes in and asks all kinds of interesting evaluative questions about the status of those assumptions.

But if we can do that to scientists and to people who write art and so forth, then we ought to, just out of sheer consistency, take seriously the same questions about our own business. What are we, as philosophers, taking for granted when we approach a certain kind of problem in a certain kind of way? What assumptions are driving the approach? What kind of conception do we have of what would be an interesting problem to look at, how might we address the problem, what would count as an adequate solution to it, and so on and so forth?

So if someone then comes along and starts dealing out those assumptions and subjecting them to critical evaluation, that ought to appear as simply a philosopher being consistently philosophical, being philosophical about his own philosophy. And that is the way I think about post-analytic philosophy, it's the way I think about Wittgenstein, it's the way I think about Heidegger.

But, of course, one could say that is just what marks any genuinely modern philosopher. What they do is precisely problematise their relation to the tradition. That makes Wittgenstein, Heidegger and the post-analytic philosophers look rather less eccentric or unusual or idiosyncratic in what they do. It just looks as if this is a perfectly natural part of the philosophical repertoire.

I don't know how much is in a name, but is 'post-analytic' the most suitable name for this tradition, and, if so, is that because, of the various traditions around today, the analytic one has become the most content with its own status?

I don't think that there's anything unique or peculiar in analytical philosophy in what one might think of as a certain lack of method-ological self-consciousness. I think the same thing could probably be said of a lot of other traditions in the history of the subject and indeed about the history of the subject as a whole. I wouldn't want to put analytical philosophy particularly in the dock, partly because that was the tradition I was brought up in, the one I'm most familiar with and sensitive to about these things. I imagine that someone brought up in the French and German traditions of philosophy might have a similarly critical view of their own, as, for example, Derrida does of phenomen-ology. These would be traditions they think have fundamentally gone wrong somewhere, but they're still the traditions they identify them-selves with. So I don't see anything more than an issue of geographical and historical contingency in that.

It's quite clear that you're not advocating a general throwing out of all that's been analytical philosophy. But if there's one respect in

which it has gone wrong most seriously, what would you identify it as?

I suppose the idea I'd come back to is the kind of criticism Kierkegaard makes of the Hegelian tradition as he inherited it. The trouble with philosophy is that philosophers seem to have an almost inveterate tendency to forget that they're human beings too. For perfectly understandable reasons, philosophers – not specifically, but including analytical philosophers – tend to forget that they are situated human beings, that they are inheritors of a particular tradition, a particular historical and cultural context, and they're responding to questions and deploying methods that themselves have a history of a more or less interesting kind. The kind of situation they find themselves in is not just a cultural or historical one. It has to do with what kind of awareness they have of what they're doing when they philosophise. When Kierkegaard makes this point about Hegel, what he's trying to bring out is the fact that Hegel is telling a certain kind of story about the history of western culture which looks as if it could only be told from a point of view outside that whole history, in other words, that it's literally a God's eye view.

It's that sense of the philosophical subject as floating free of embeddedness, context and situation that Kierkegaard is worried about. One way of summarising that aspect of context or situatedness is to leave it as a reminder to philosophy that there is a literary aspect or dimension to what philosophers do. It's not that philosophers aren't at all aware of that fact. But it's that they might not be giving as much thought to the implications of it as it might be worth giving.

Many people working in British universities are quite happy with analytic philosophy and don't see any particular need for post-analytic philosophy. So how do you see things playing out there?

I wouldn't say there is any sense in which philosophy has gone post-analytic. Certainly not in the UK. Three things I think are true. I think that it's certainly the case that more UK philosophy departments take seriously the need to have at least someone who can teach French and German philosophy. That began a while ago, but I think that's very rightly continuing. I also think there is a lot of evidence that the kinds of reading of Wittgenstein we've been talking about, associated more with Cavell, Diamond and figures of that kind, are increasingly popular.

I also think that people like Taylor, Murdoch, Nussbaum and so on, have a pretty well established place in the subject. When one is thinking about issues in political philosophy, moral philosophy and so on, I think these people are taken seriously, and I don't see any prospect of that disappearing altogether. I suppose from my point of view what is missing is a sense of the way these bits might fit together, a sense of the picture they might paint of the subject as a whole, if you put them together in the kinds of ways I am interested in doing. The idea of philosophy as having a lot of separate branches or subsectors begins to crack if you take what Diamond and Murdoch say about politics and ethics seriously. And that would radically alter the way we think of philosophy across the board, not just within these evaluative ghettos. That's something that it seems to me is worth getting out and debating.

What about your own work? A lot of it has been associated with Cavell. Do you see your own work continuing in that vein or will there be a new direction for you?

It's the classic, almost psychoanalytic, problem in philosophy that you no sooner kill one father than you've got another one to worry about. The problem in finding in someone like Cavell a way of getting out from under a particular kind of interpretation of Wittgenstein is that you then run the risk of just finding yourself reiterating, ventriloquising, the new way of reading Wittgenstein. There's obviously a sense in which what I very self-consciously tried to do in the book on Cavell was to find or help create a wider audience for a way of reading Wittgenstein that I thought was exceptionally interesting and important. To that degree, I was explicitly, deliberately, subordinating my own voice to his, in ways which I think would trouble people who take Cavell seriously, precisely because for him a loss of voice of that kind is a rather worrying thing. So it is absolutely essential to me that I do something else, that without denying the importance of that inheritance, I find a way of going on with it that allows me to do what I want to do in and with philosophy that is more than exegetical in its relation to Cavell.

There's a book due out with OUP, where I'm at least trying to find a certain kind of distance for my own interests and preoccupations from his. But that means it begins by going rather more deeply into some of his preoccupations and interests. Whether it will be obvious to the people who read it that it's as much a distancing, as it is a deepening, of my relationship to Cavell is very unclear.

Select Bibliography

On Film, Routledge, 2002

Inheritance and Originality: Wittgenstein, Heidegger, Kierkegaard, Oxford University Press, 2001

The Cavell Reader, Blackwell, 1996

Stanley Cavell: Philosophy's Recounting of the Ordinary, Oxford University Press, 1994

Faith and Reason, Duckworth, 1994

15 A Post-Human Hell

In conversation with Keith Ansell Pearson

In a passage in his book, *The Blind Watchmaker*, written in the middle of the 1980s, Richard Dawkins speculates about some far-off time in the future, where intelligent computers ponder their own lost origins. He wonders whether they will hit on the truth that they sprang from an earlier, organic, carbon-based form of life. He even imagines that one of them might write a book called *Electronic Takeover*. However, he concludes that this kind of speculation is the stuff of science fiction, and that it probably sounds a bit far-fetched.

Had Dawkins been able to fast-forward some 15 years to visit Tilehurst Surgery in Reading on 24 August 1998, at 4:00 p.m., he might have had second thoughts about the improbability of his scenario. He would have found Kevin Warwick, Professor of Cybernetics at Reading University, being operated on to implant a silicon chip transponder in his arm. By the mechanism of this transponder, Warwick spent nine days being able to use lights, doors, heaters and computers without touching them. So bullish is Warwick about the future of this kind of technology, that he has been led to declare: 'I was born human. But this was an accident of fate – a condition merely of time and place. I believe it's something we have the power to change'.

The idea that intelligent machine-life might come to supplant organic based human-life is not a new one. It is, after all, a theme which has been explored many times in movies, on television and in comic books. However, the possibility is now being taken seriously by the professionals working in the field of artificial intelligence. This is partly to do with thoughts about Moore's Law, which describes the growth rate of computer processing power. If Moore's Law holds true over the next few decades (there is a doubt about this which has to do with the limits of miniaturisation), it seems that computers will have the processing power of the human brain by 2050, at the latest. Significantly, there is no reason why the increase in processing power will stop there. The belief is that machines will rapidly outstrip humans in this capacity.

It is important to understand that processing power does not equate to intelligence or consciousness. Indeed, some people, such as Roger Penrose, doubt whether a genuinely artificial, computational intelligence will ever be possible. However, for other thinkers, it is only a matter of time before increased processing power is harnessed to create genuinely intelligent machines. For example, Warwick in *March of the Machines* argues that it is ridiculous to think that machines won't surpass humans in their intelligence. Similarly, Hans Moravec, a founder of the robotics department at Carnegie Mellon University, predicts that by 2040 machines will match human intelligence, and possibly consciousness, and that thereafter they will become more advanced than humans.

How we should feel about this prospect is not clear. Some people look forward to the advent of a 'post-human' existence. Marvin Minsky, for example, argues that nanotechnology will enable human beings to replace their brains entirely. Once freed from the constraints of biology we will be able to make choices about the length of our lives and develop other unimaginable capabilities. He claims that robots *will* inherit the earth, but they will be our children. It is our duty, he argues, to make sure that this happens, because that way we see to it that the struggle for life called evolution does not end up in a meaningless waste.

Other thinkers are much more suspicious about the idea of a post-human future. Keith Ansell Pearson forms part of this group. He argues that it is necessary to reclaim the future for philosophy, rescuing it from the futurologists and cyber-gurus. The notion that we have no choice but to resign ourselves to a future where we are outwitted by super-intelligent machines must be resisted. Moreover, for him, living in a post-human world would be like living in a hell where one is condemned to eternal life and complete transparency.

Has philosophy always been an interest of yours?

Well actually, I went to University to study history. Philosophy as an academic discipline seemed a very alien world to me, my interests were those of a social outsider. I had this overwhelming sense of being completely alienated from society. At the time I didn't suspect a philosophy department could provide a home for someone like me. I've always had what one might loosely describe as a metaphysical bent, but back then I was too impatient to bother with the academic study of philosophy. I wanted to change the world, not interpret it!

So given that you weren't at that point interested in philosophy, what were your intellectual interests?

My interests were philosophical but not in any academically respectable or conventional sense. There were two main currents influencing me, sometimes producing unbearable tensions, but which ultimately expressed themselves in that I became what I suppose one could call a 'left Nietzschean'. On the one hand, I was interested in Marxian thought – Marcuse was my hero as a young person and his *One Dimensional-Man* was the text through which I saw the world – and, on the other, I was into what I would call 'outsider literature' – the usual suspects, such as Dostoevsky and company. I was reading Nietzsche at this time but not in an academic context. I did my final year dissertation on Marx's role in the First International. After graduating I decided to take a year off in which I took German classes and read a lot of philosophy. I had won two book prizes for my degree and I remember buying Russell's *Problems of Philosophy* and Kant's *Critique of Pure Reason*. But during that year I devoted most of my time to reading Marxist literature, all the classic texts such as those by Lukács, Korsch, Gramsci, Colletti, Benjamin and Adorno, and so on.

After considering various options, I decided to go to Sussex, at that time known as a centre of Marxist philosophy and social theory, with the aim of doing a thesis on Walter Benjamin and Marxism. During the MA things evolved somewhat differently and I ended up writing a lot of work on Nietzsche, notably his *Genealogy of Morals*. This was a time when Nietzsche was becoming a key reference point for a lot of diverse trajectories of thought, and shortly after this period the whole Nietzsche industry came into action and an astonishing number and array of books were published and continue to be published. It was quite extraordinary, from being a complete non-person in philosophy departments, Nietzsche became a thinker who eclipsed Marx in intellectual debates. I was not entirely comfortable with the eclipse of Marx by Nietzsche, and sought to cultivate a left Nietzscheanism.

So what did you see as being involved in this left Nietzscheanism?
Well, it is perhaps a curious hybrid. My sense of it was not simply intellectual, it emerged out of the background I came from, a 1970s background of a working class kid heavily into the alternative music

scene of the time and very much a disaffected youth. The revolution could not be a mere social revolution, improving living conditions and creating a more just society; it had to be about creating the conditions that would give rise to qualitatively different and new human beings. It had to overcome both psychic repression and social alienation. It's in this context that I encountered a collection of thinkers I could readily identify with: Marcuse, Adorno, Bataille, Deleuze, Foucault, all of whom could be read, in their differing ways, as left Nietzscheans. It was a terribly un-English education and absolutely outside of the analytic establishment.

So do you think it was your sense of isolation and alienation that attracted you to thinkers who might loosely be termed 'continental', rather than to their analytic counterparts?

Yes, definitely. 'Continental' philosophy, as it became called, had a radicality about it that appealed to me. It allowed you to intimately connect your philosophical practice with other crucial aspects of your existence. For me the feeling was that philosophy could contribute to what used to be called 'the revolution of everyday life'. At places like Warwick and Essex, the two main centres where continental philosophy was studied in the 1980s, it suddenly became possible to do serious philosophical work on people like Adorno, Foucault, Levinas, Lyotard, Irigaray, Derrida, Deleuze, etc., and although one was doing philosophical work such work was informed by existential and political commitments, be they feminist or Marxist. The establishment of so-called 'centres of excellence' in continental philosophy provided, and continues to provide, a home for many people who are driven to do philosophy because of these commitments and because they think philosophy has a role to play in shaping them. Now, some people, perhaps of a more analytic persuasion, regard a lot of the work done in this area as being typically pretentious and portentous. This is a criticism I regard as intellectually smug. It's also, in my view, ethically deficient. As something of a Marxist I would almost be tempted to say it's the ideology of the ruling class. Someone might say, it's simply the view of common sense, but then for me common sense is part of this ideology!

I think the situation is changing in that there is now much more intellectual mobility taking place between the two traditions and students and graduates are being encouraged to draw on the resources that both have to offer. This is certainly true of my experience at Warwick. Clearly, there are differences between the way the two traditions practise philosophy: differences of style and approach, for example. But it is not as if one of these traditions has a monopoly on standards of rigour and clarity, or even profundity.

I actually see myself as something of a philosophy outsider. Some of the thinkers I'm most interested in simply don't figure in the canon of continental philosophy. Bergson, who has largely been erased from our appreciation of twentieth-century philosophy, is a good example here. He is not someone the majority of continental philosophers read or seem to know how to read; and Deleuze, whose first book was on Hume and empiricism, is difficult to place and situate as a continental figure. As for Nietzsche, well, he is the philosopher outsider par excellence, but everyone reads him these days!

Your interest in Nietzsche is central to your book *Viroid Life*, where you explore the relationship between biotechnology and the future of the human being. You make great play out of the notion of the 'transhuman condition'. What do you take the transhuman condition to be?

In advocating the transhuman, I was trying to expose the hollowness of the 'post-human', which seemed to be the way the postmodern condition was now getting construed. Here the claim was that with the rise of AI, robotics, and cyber culture, the human was now becoming post-human. This was also coupled with claims about evolution, ones being made not only by populist cyber-writers and gurus like Kevin Kelly, but also by eminent scientists such as David Deutsch in his *The Fabric of Reality*. It is entertained as a serious thesis about evolution. Evolution is becoming self-directed, a kind of Lamarckian takeover of blind and dumb natural selection. In Kelly the claim is that evolution has been searching for something like the human brain in order to speed itself up and achieve a self-directedness, not because it – evolution – is anthropomorphic but because speed is the runaway circuit upon which it rides. In Deutsch, the premise is that if you accept that entropy is the problem presented to life on a macroscopic level then it is legitimate to say that knowledge-bearing systems are the telos of evolution. I see this as a new Darwinism, a technological Darwinism replacing social Darwinism, but just as intellectually dubious and politically pernicious. So I wanted to reclaim the future for philosophy and from the futurologists and our cyber-gurus.

I'm not clear why you take this new Darwinism to be intellectually dubious and politically pernicious?

It's intellectually dubious because there is no substantive empirical basis to its claims. How do we know what evolution is up to, supposing it is up to anything? Should we even speak of 'evolution' as if it was an entity? It's interesting to note that Darwin himself never used the term except once at the very end of his *Origin of Species*. It is politically pernicious in that like social Darwinism it falls into the trap of reading a narrow conception of nature or *bios* into something which is not nature or *bios*, transposing the implacable laws of natural selection – namely, the survival of the fittest, which is now extended to technology and the becoming of matter itself – into the specifically historical and cultural and, as a result, conflating processes that are quite distinct.

So what form does your critique take?

Well, there are a number of elements to it. First, it is possible to show that this ideology of the future contributes to a legitimation of late-modern capital. Capital is now in the business of selling the future to us, including selling us our souls, it is in our heads and minds. I remember an interview in *Wired* between a journalist and Daniel Dennett in which the main discussion was whether or not we should assign rights to machines. I found this discussion grotesque: we live in a world where a great mass of the human beings on the planet live in conditions of poverty, squalor, and starvation. They do not even belong to a level of material and social organisation where 'rights' could be assigned to them and be meaningful to them. I should say, of course, that it is perfectly legitimate for philosophers to discuss and raise questions about 'rights' – animal rights, machine rights, and so on, but we need to appreciate that our treatment of rights with respect to these things tells us more about our own predicaments than it does about the animal in itself or the machine in itself. Neither can such an issue as the rights of machines be raised naively without an appreciation of some wider context which is informing it, such as, I would suggest, global late-modern capitalism.

Second, I want to propose, in response to notions of the post-human, a transvaluation of values. I regard post-human thinking as a technological Darwinism because its values are solely those of efficiency and utility: the talk is all about acquiring bigger and faster memories, downloading our brains, creating a non-culture of learning in which we learn a foreign language by putting chips into our neuronal circuit. It's an insidious new form of social control and normalization.

And finally, I think it is important to deflate the claims being made on behalf of the post-human future. One can show that there is nothing new about it. Samuel Butler published an essay in the 1860s entitled *Darwin Among the Machines* – the title is significant – which argued that the future would be one of machine takeover and that with the dominance of machines we would face the prospect of these machines deciding our fate, for instance by exterminating us. The scenario envisaged is one of a technological survival of the fittest and, of course, the machines win hands down. This is the kind of scenario now being proposed by Kevin Warwick, who runs the cybernetics outfit at Reading University. Also, one can interrogate the claim that the human is now embarked upon a post-biological evolution by arguing that the human has, for the greatest part of its history, always been a post-biological creature. The history of the human animal is nothing other than the history of a post-biological becoming mediated by social and technical machines. I should perhaps stress that my argument is not an argument against technology – whatever that would amount to.

Much of the language of your critique of this ideology of the post-human is couched in terms of notions of human becoming and overcoming, and you also refer to the 'sickness' of man's present condition. I recognise the Nietzschean antecedents here, but what exactly is involved in these ideas?

Well, Nietzsche thinks that the human condition is precisely to overcome itself. We continually remake ourselves. So he would say that if you look back on the history of human societies and religions, their moral practices, social practices and their customs, then you'll see that certain human types were created. And you can change the human type. You can create a culture in which drives are internalised, where people have a bad conscience about their natural drives and instincts, or you can create a culture where people sublimate them in a completely different fashion. For Nietzsche the only law of life is one of self-overcoming.

He's asking us to be honest with ourselves and to evolve with the aid of an intellectual conscience, which means experimenting upon ourselves and inventing practices of truth that will facilitate this. Nietzsche is essentially a non-Darwinian thinker, one who knows and has learnt the lessons of Darwin – that Darwinism is on one level 'correct' – but there is the desire to propose new visions and riddles of what it is to be human, to become human, to become *overhuman*. This isn't about easing the cultural tasks of human existence but about cultivating new creative techniques and practices of the self, as Foucault came to call them, experimenting on the body and the soul, creating new affects, new sensations, new perceptions. Nietzsche examines the cultures and religions of the past precisely in these terms: what kind of human, what types of human, did they create? If God is dead, then what new kinds of human beings can be created now? He did not think that you could deliberately fashion and 'breed' new types of being, but you could create the conditions that might prove favourable to their emergence. We still live in a society that cannot tolerate real variation and difference and which endlessly perpetuates the one image as a dominant image: that of *man*.

You mention that Nietzsche is essentially a non-Darwinian thinker, and in *Viroid Life* you talk about the fact that he is sceptical about the possibility that the new human type might emerge straight-forwardly out of a process of Darwinian natural selection. What explains this scepticism? Why is the emergence of the transhuman type problematic?

Well, at one level, the notion of the transhuman directs our attention to the possibilities of the human, indicating tasks of self-overcoming which we can incorporate into our social and intellectual practices. This question of incorporation is very important for Nietzsche. Our becoming transhuman does not come about through a process of natural selection, this is to misunderstand the point – Nietzsche's point – completely. It's got nothing to do with our genetic endowment since this bestows so little in terms of what we might become. In fact, this is bound up with issues that both Nietzsche and Bergson deal with – particularly, the need to provide a generative account of the human condition as an evolutionary condition, which means that you ask questions such as: Why do we have the mental habits of representation we do? Why do we perceive the world in the way we do? Why do we think in spatial rather than durational terms? And the answers that Nietzsche and Bergson give to this set of questions are strikingly similar: because our evolutionary condition is primarily one of adaptation and this compels us to relate to matter in ways that serve to satisfy our practical needs and interests.

But then the philosophical task is one of opening up this existence and its possibilities by seeking to 'think beyond the human condition'. We have a paradox: on the one hand, the human animal is the machine that has broken with its mechanistic conditions of existence, broken free of the circle of animal closure; but on the other hand it exists in a 'closed society' and produces a 'closed morality' – and in such a state of closure, human beings act in accordance with obligations they are not expected to comprehend and obey authorities that are arbitrary. How then we do we create new possibilities of existence, new forms of life? What new perceptions of space and time might be available to us? Can we explore how we become human by also becoming other than and more than human, what Nietzsche called overhuman? This is a different kind of 'deterritorialization' (or transformation) to the one effected by capital. This is the crucial point.

You mentioned earlier the necessity to resist and find alternatives to a post-human future that is predicated upon values solely of efficiency and utility. In your book you talk about the 'hell' of living life beyond illusion, of living in pure immediacy and total transparency. I'm certain that some people won't see the problem in this kind of future, so what's your objection?

Well, let me answer this in terms of a truly remarkable essay Lyotard wrote in the 1980s that got ignored by virtually everyone. It is on the 'inhuman' and in this essay – or what became a set of essays – he asks after *two* inhumans: the inhuman of technological development – where capital is construed as the vehicle or carrier of an inhuman destiny, one of mere evolutionary survival and development in which what drives technology is the need to create intelligent machines which will survive the extinction of the sun; and another 'inhuman' which we might call a 'philosophical' one. This philosophical 'inhuman' is bound up with the stranger within and the concern is how the first inhuman, in triumphing over all other realities and possibilities of evolution, cancels out or erases this stranger, this second inhuman.

In essence, Lyotard's concern is whether the machines of the future will have *affective* memories as well as *effective* memories. As he says, 'I am not interested in survival, I am interested in remaining a child'. It's a sentimental thought, deliberately and provocatively so, but also strangely beautiful and profound. Remaining a child in this context, let me stress, does not mean preserving a state of innocence and ignorance, a state uncontaminated and uncorrupted by knowledge; rather it provides the conditions by which meaningful self-knowledge can be developed and have any affect on us.

his last published book, which carried the deceptively simple and old-fashioned title, *What is Philosophy?*, Deleuze noted that we appear to lack a will to creation and a resistance to the present. There seems to be a great deal of fatalism and resignationism infecting what used to be known as the radical intelligentsia with respect to this issue. Post-modern politics is all about fragmentation and particularism, and the depressing thing I witnessed in the 1990s was all these different groups competing and fighting, as if present at some Darwinian banquet, only for their particular vision of the future, each one declaring: the future is mine!

The really key issue is the one concerning time. What does time mean to us today? Have we run out of time? Are we simply adapting to a future that is given to us, a kind of time of the future in which everything is given in advance and which is not, therefore, a time at all? I would go so far as to say that philosophy thinks time and thinks nothing else. When we think the being of the past and the being of the future we have expanded our conception of the present, and our sense of the horizon, including the horizon of possibilities, has changed. Life involves the coexistence of heterogeneous durations. In my view, current cyber-discourse on technology does not allow for this kind of thinking on time; it's as if we have indeed 'run out of time', we have no choice but to adapt to an alien future in which our fate is to be outwitted by so-called intelligent machines. But this contains no thinking of time as an event – except in terms of our extinction, but strange as it may sound, this would not be an event. Going back to Deleuze's last book: for me what is significant about it is its attempt to draw and uphold a distinction between philosophy as 'absolute deterritorialization' and capital as 'relative deterritorialization'. The only problem, of course, is that the power of philosophy to change the world is a very limited one compared with the actual powers that really do change the world. You see, I'm still stuck in the dilemma of Marx's eleventh thesis on Feuerbach! I don't think I'm the only one.

Taking a slightly different view on these issues, there seems to be an interesting parallel between some of the ideas that you put forward – I'm thinking here, for example, of your rejection of humanism, your view that there is no permanent human essence, and the kinds of references that you make to the 'sickness' of the human condition – and the way in which you describe some of the experiences of your youth. I know that it is possible to oversimplify these things, but do you think that there are any significant correspondences here?

For sure there are. I have no problem with being a 'sick animal'. However, I very much subscribe to the way in which Nietzsche conceives of how one becomes what one is: namely, one must not have the *faintest* idea what one is. It's a remarkable paradox, a deeply uncanny truth about the self. If one has an adequate conception of becoming, which requires having an adequate conception of time, then Nietzsche's statement makes perfect sense. We are essentially unknown to ourselves and the world is essentially unknown to us. This doesn't mean we have to invoke the ineffable or appeal to the mystery of life. While I recognise the incredible force of Wittgenstein's closing statement in the *Tractatus* – of that which we cannot speak we should remain silent – I hold to the exact contrary view: philosophy exists to give expression to that which we think we can only remain silent about. This, for me, is a crucial aspect of what philosophy does. It's close perhaps to painting and music, but it's unique in that it works with concepts, which it creates as events or possible worlds.

To answer your question more directly and less obliquely: there is no doubt that I was drawn to philosophers like Nietzsche and Deleuze out of a certain existential compulsion. There is a history of madness in my family and the most formative event of my early childhood was my father's mental illness – he was diagnosed as suffering from 'paranoid schizophrenia' when I was five. It cannot be denied that this forms a crucial component of my particular existence, including my philosophical existence. It's a definite wound in my being. Some of my books are of great personal significance for me, especially *Germinal Life*, but although it treats some fairly deep, complex, and strange areas of existence, and philosophises about things like the wound and the crack-up of life, it's most definitely not philosophy as confession, therapy, or literature. I want to insist upon this. I don't approach philosophy in the vain hope of discovering or finding myself and I don't believe one writes for oneself – one writes for the other, including the other that is oneself. The self is something completely vertiginous. There is only becoming. This is the profound and uncanny truth of time.

Select Bibliography

Philosophy and the Adventure of the Virtual: Bergson and the Time of Life, Routledge, 2001

Germinal Life: The Difference and Repetition of Deleuze, Routledge, 1999

Viroid Life: Perspectives on Nietzsche and the Transhuman Condition, Routledge, 1997

Deleuze and Philosophy. The Difference Engineer (editor), Routledge, 1997

'Life becoming body: on the "meaning" of post human evolution', *Cultural Values*, 1: 2, 1997

16   Philosophy and the Public

In conversation with Nigel Warburton

The book you are reading is an example of a genre with a chequered history. It is a book about serious philosophy, as pursued in our great universities, which aims to be of interest not only to those immersed in the subject, but to general readers as well.

It may seem somewhat surprising, but historically many have wondered whether it is even possible for such a book to succeed in its goals. Despite some notable exceptions, not much serious work on philosophy was written with the general reader in mind in the Britain of the twentieth century, especially in the forty or so years after the Second World War. When people like Bertrand Russell wrote his 'pot boilers' for the mass market, his professional colleagues sneered with derision (though whether this was because of their nature or quality is a matter for debate).

In recent years, the tide has begun to turn. Major philosophers such as Daniel Dennett, John Searle, Thomas Nagel and Simon Blackburn have written books which can be picked up and read by any reasonably intelligent reader, regardless of whether or not they have any philosophical training.

At the same time, some best-selling books on philosophy have been written by non-academics, most notably Jostein Gaarder's *Sophie's World* and Alain de Botton's *The Consolations of Philosophy*, which was also a successful television series.

This change has not been an entirely unproblematic development. John Searle, for example, describes writing for a popular market as 'a tremendous intellectual discipline', adding that, 'In general I feel if you can't say it clearly you don't understand it yourself'. But he also cautioned that 'you do pay a price for stating it simply, namely it's easier for the professionals to misunderstand it'. With simplicity comes a loss of detail, and that's often where crucial philosophical work takes place.

It is also arguable that some of the other best-selling philosophy books don't accurately reflect the subject at all, a concern which Nigel Warburton raises in this interview.

The issue is close to Warburton's heart since it is as a populariser of philosophy that he has become best known. He is also in a position to experience another downside of popular writing, namely, that it can obscure the author's more academic work. As well as being a populariser, Warburton has published serious academic work in aesthetics and applied ethics. Yet his profile as a writer of popular books means that his more academic output tends to fall under its shadow, and one can easily get a skewed image of Warburton as a writer who only publishes for the popular market.

The populariser occupies an important role as the link between academic philosophy and the wider public; a relationship which has not been close in recent years. While many academic scientists and historians in particular have successfully brought their subjects to the wider world, their philosophical colleagues have not been so engaged. This can't simply be a matter of philosophy being complex, since some of the most successful works of popular science have dealt with quantum physics, which is about as difficult a subject as one could find. So it is hard to see how the relative dearth of popular writing by eminent philosophers could be explained by the nature of philosophy itself. The real explanation must lie elsewhere.

The appetite among the public for philosophy has been demonstrated by the success of those few books which have been addressed to it. This poses several questions for academic philosophers. Are they going to satisfy this appetite or are they going to leave it for others, perhaps less qualified, to do it for them? And if it can and should be done, are there risks and dangers? If so can they be avoided?

These are all questions which have occupied Nigel Warburton and which he addresses in this interview.

You are best known for your popular writing. Your first such book was *Philosophy: The Basics*. What made you decide to write that book?

In the final year of my Ph.D., I was surviving almost entirely from teaching, mostly A-level philosophy. I was aware that there weren't many good introductions to philosophy. Apart from John Hospers' book, Bertrand Russell's rather dated *The Problems of Philosophy* and *Philosophy Made Simple*, there really weren't any good, clear introductions that students could follow. I was very aware of that because I would have liked to have used one in my teaching. So I found myself writing my own notes, which I would pass on to students to support the teaching. It was an easy transition from that to writing the notes up into a book. That process was actually very useful because the year I was writing *Philosophy: The Basics*, I was teaching about twenty-five hours a week in term time. I needed to have the teaching materials well thought out to be effective as a teacher; it also gave me a chance to try out the material to see if students could follow it or not.

I got a contract for the book on the basis of a specimen chapter and an outline. I wrote most of it from 1989–90. I was living in London, just about surviving from odd teaching jobs and working on a stall in

Covent Garden Market at the weekends to make ends meet. It sounds absurd, but I didn't have enough money to print out the whole book from my Amstrad. I saw the introductory book, *Philosophy: The Basics*, as a way of consolidating my teaching, but also as a way into getting a job in philosophy too, as it showed I could teach philosophy. That was naive because that's not the main criterion for getting a philosophy job in Britain. The absurd situation is that you're employed predominantly to teach philosophy, but you're selected primarily on your ability to publish research in peer-reviewed journals – an activity which doesn't require particularly developed communication skills.

Is it the case that writing popular philosophy is undervalued and not sufficiently encouraged? If so, it is still, presumably, a rewarding enough activity.

It does bring its own rewards, in two ways. One reward is that it's much more widely read than any research. *Philosophy: The Basics* is now in its eighth translation and third edition and many thousands of copies have been read. *Thinking from A to Z* and *Philosophy: The Classics* have both gone into second editions too. I get feedback from people who have read my books, and that's very gratifying in itself. The other reward is financial because obviously if you sell a large number of copies, it increases your income, and also your ability to command better royalties and advances on subsequent books. But within the academic philosophical community, it tends to be sneered upon by some people as not serious, not the real thing. It has played a role in my getting jobs, but it's certainly not something that has counted highly in promotion.

Isn't there an argument that for many philosophers this kind of work should be encouraged more, as it's actually a better use of their time?

As I see it, there are very few philosophers a century that make an impact on the subject – perhaps one or two a decade. That's just the way it is. Most of the philosophers who are alive today and writing prolifically will be completely forgotten in twenty, maybe thirty years. Probably sooner than that. Only a handful will make a serious impact on the subject. There's a great deal of self-deception about what is going on in universities. From an undergraduate's point of view, you have people who are reluctant teachers, because they always want to get back to their research. All the pressure is on lecturers to do their very serious research, which is demanding all their intellectual energy and it's an annoyance to have to deal with the students. So the students get inferior teaching as a result of that.

From the lecturer's point of view, many of them see themselves as philosophers making highly original and important additions to the subject. Sadly, most of them are making fairly banal, footnote-like contributions to what has become an industry for churning out articles and books as an end in itself. These are scarcely read. That's not surprising when you see how poorly written many of them are. Usually they are something to bulk up a CV. I want to make it clear that I am not denigrating all research in philosophy – it *can* be intellectually stimulating, it *can* be valuable, it's probably a necessary condition of the few geniuses emerging from this mass of mediocrity. But to do that at the expense of teaching students? Philosophy is a wonderful subject that can transform people's lives. But it needs to be well taught. Often what happens is that because of this selfish, self-deceptive attitude of 'I'm a serious researcher making a massive contribution to my subject', we're depriving students of good teaching in the subject.

If I had to describe my mission within academic philosophy, I'd say it's to be a serious educator. I do want to carry on doing my own research, but I'm not naive enough to think that it is worthwhile to devote myself entirely to my research. I don't want to be another obscure footnote in an academic journal (actually I already *am* an obscure footnote in several journals). I'm more ambitious for myself, and given my record of communicating philosophy to a wider audience, the best use of my time within philosophy is surely to reach a wider audience. If as part of my personal development I want to do research that's fine, but I shouldn't be under the delusion that this is going to make a tremendous impact on the subject or on the few people who read it. I don't think I'm unique, or even particularly unusual in being in this position: I think most philosophers would be better off devoting a substantial part of their life and energy to teaching the subject. Research in philosophy is not like research in some other subjects: in philosophy mediocre research has no value at all. It's not cumulative in the way some of the sciences can be, where lesser researchers can contribute as part of a team.

Is this something which you came to think about later or was it the guiding principle which led you to follow up the success of *The Basics* with more work like that?

It's been a gradual, emerging revelation to me. When I was beginning my Ph.D., like all Ph.D. students, I thought I was going to make a serious contribution to philosophy, because that's what you are encouraged to think, and for all I knew maybe I would. But I looked and saw what happened. I had read other people's research. I had seen the books that emerged from research students and saw that it can actually be an extremely stultifying subject when it is turned into this business of academia. I don't think that philosophy needs to be kept within the walls of academia. And I think it should be very far from a business. There is a risk that in an age of scholastic obscurity, philosophy will wither as an academic subject within universities and will grow and metamorphose outside of universities. In publishing, there are signs that this is happening, with the success of *Sophie's World* and *The Consolations of Philosophy*. These are in the best-sellers lists. Most people reading these are way outside academic philosophy and the people writing them are outside academic philosophy too. The result is that the popular view of our subject is that it is either a kind of awe at the world, or a kind of self-help therapy. I'd rather see philosophy popularised by people with a firm grounding in the subject. Otherwise there is a risk that what is most valuable about it will be lost. Unfortunately, many of those who are in a position to portray philosophy at its best to a wider audience see this activity as somehow beneath them, despite the precedents of David Hume and Bertrand Russell.

You're suggesting that there is a neglect among professional philosophers for the wider audience and that as a result non-professional philosophers are taking up the challenge to write popular philosophy. What do you think we risk losing as a result of this process?

Well, let's take the loss to the philosophers. The classical conception of a philosopher is someone who thinks about their own life, as well as about the nature of life. You wonder about the competence of some people who, having thought about their own lives, have decided to devote them entirely to making a mediocre contribution to an obscure debate. It's like deciding to spend your life solving crossword puzzles. These people are the best philosophers, in the sense that they've passed all the exams and their peers say they're the best philosophers, but are they really in the spirit of philosophy when they do this?

What do you make of the accusation that, in order to reach a wider audience, standards must slip?

I'm not arguing that you should dumb down philosophy in order to reach the largest possible audience. But I am maintaining that there are many people who are intellectually sophisticated, who are eager to find out about philosophy, but who find a brick wall of technical terms and obscurity when they try to find out more, and consequently, they look somewhere else. There's no reason why there shouldn't be a way in for them. There are more and more of these books, radio and television programmes giving people access to quite highbrow subjects. Ten or fifteen years ago that wasn't true. Now there are a mass of them, some of which are excellent. There are some writers doing the same job for philosophy, but not enough.

People often talk about popular works of philosophy as though this were one genre. You identify several genres that could all come under the broad heading of popularisations. What are they?

There are at least four ways in which you can popularise philosophy. One is the way people like Daniel Dennett do it, which is to write original philosophy in an accessible and entertaining style. That's quite rare. There are few skilled practitioners who can pull it off in the way Richard Dawkins does for zoology. The second way is what I call the sugared pill: sweetening the philosophy with something more palatable. *Sophie's World* and *The Consolations of Philosophy* are two examples of this. *Sophie's World* tells a story and puts the philosophy over through that. *The Consolations of Philosophy* turns the philosophy into therapy, and it's the self-help therapy that moves you into the philosophy. Inevitably if you include a great deal of sugar there isn't much room for the philosophy. Another genre is biography, which is a further way to sugar the pill, telling the life story of philosophers and slipping in the philosophy along the way. The two outstanding exponents of that genre are Ray Monk, particularly in his biography of Wittgenstein, and Ben Rogers, who has written a biography of A. J. Ayer. Their books exploit the fact that most people are more interested in the private lives of philosophers than in their public thoughts. A fourth genre is the straight introduction, like my *Philosophy: The Basics*.

You said earlier that the goal is not to dumb down when writing popular philosophy. What are the difficulties in writing clearly but accurately about philosophy in such a way that somebody who doesn't know anything about the subject can follow it and gain something from it?

It seems to me that there are surprisingly few people who can write clearly about the subject without distorting it so much that serious practitioners of the subject feel it's being trivialised. People who have done it well recently include Stephen Law with *The Philosophy Files*, and Simon Blackburn with *Think*. They feel that they ought to be doing this. But very few who try it, manage to pull it off. I really don't know why. Maybe they think it's easier than it is. But it's not *that* difficult and there are rules you can follow. George Orwell has got an excellent list of rules in his essay 'Politics and the English Language', so have Strunk and White in *The Elements of Style*. If you follow these, people will understand what you're saying.

Some people argue that philosophy is hopelessly impoverished without detailed and focused argumentation, and that the problem of popular philosophy is precisely that it has to do away with this kind of detail. Presumably you don't subscribe to this view.

It's not an obvious problem. The point of an introductory book is not to be a substitute for the study of philosophy. It's to be an aid, an inspiration, a support. It's supposed to lead people to the real thing. But it can only rarely be the real thing itself. In my introductory books, I'm not aiming to provide the equivalent of an injection that can painlessly give you everything you need to know about philosophy. I aim to give people a sample so that they can go from never having studied the subject, to understanding enough of it to see whether they want to go further – to see which routes they might want to take in the subject. *Philosophy: The Classics*, for instance, consists of 24 short introductions to classic texts in the history of philosophy from Plato through to Rawls. The point of that book isn't to be an alternative to reading those philosophy books, though it could serve that if you were short of time. My main purpose is to inspire people to go and read some of these classic works, having a critical overview of what sort of ideas are contained within them, and some notion of which books are likely to repay the investment of time it takes to read them.

There is a feeling, perhaps on the increase as people come to the realisation that you have to make things practical in order to get them funded, that philosophy teaches the transferable skill of critical thinking. How important do you think this is for the value of philosophy?

There are so many different things that are studied under the name of philosophy, even within British universities. Some courses are very good at training people in transferable thinking skills. It pains me to say it, but the Oxbridge tutorial, with its adversarial approach, works well in this respect. When you've got a student one-on-one with a tutor, reading out an essay and getting it savaged by a brilliant mind in an armchair (at least in principle), this provides a very good training in transferable thinking skills of a certain sort. You're constantly being made to question your assumptions, revise badly structured arguments, defend positions which you adhere to and so on. Actually, a lot of philosophy isn't taught in a way which is interactive because it's too expensive to do that generally. As a result, some students emerge from some universities with a degree in philosophy but very poor thinking skills. But ideally the subject can make a massive contribution to society by training people not only to think clearly and critically but to write succinctly and intelligently about abstract and difficult issues.

Can people get some of that pay-off by doing a little bit of philosophy or do they really need to get a thorough grounding in it before they can learn those skills?

It depends on who they are. At the Open University we get a very wide range of students and I've taught people from educationally deprived backgrounds through to people with doctorates in different subjects. Within that range I have met some who, through their work or academic studies in other areas, have developed very sophisticated thinking skills. You don't have to give them very much in philosophy to get them up to a very high level – they see the point immediately. Other people can study philosophy all their lives and not make much progress. There are huge individual differences. I have actually come across a few people who are unteachable in philosophy in the sense that they don't make any progress at all. They don't accept some of the basic methodology – they're happy to embrace contradictions, they can't distinguish coherent argument from bullshit, and so on. Philosophy is one thing and the person studying it is another. There's a wide range of things in philosophy and people come to it with diverse motivations and competence levels. I don't think there's any reason why everybody should study philosophy formally, but I think that almost everybody who ever thinks about a position will engage in philosophy at some level, whether they realise it or not. I do think it should be more widely taught in schools, though, as not everyone has the luxury of devoting time to the subject at university.

Do you think philosophy can make a real difference to people's lives?

I think philosophy is a wonderful subject and it can transform people's lives. Particularly in the first few years of studying it. It's certainly done that for me. That might sound evangelical, but I do believe that studying philosophy for two or three years has a profound effect on the way you live, how you think and particularly how you assess other people's arguments – your own too, sometimes.

How has it changed you?

One of the commonest ways in which philosophy changes people's lives is to allow them to question religion. Many people who have been brought up as religious believers have found that when they examine critically the arguments on which their fundamental expectations about life and after are based, there are no solid grounds for believing in a God of any description.

Were you a religious believer?

I have been, yes. I went through an adolescent phase of it, but fortunately I saw the light! Studying philosophy can make you more realistic about the place of superstition in people's lives.

Many people attest to the transformative power of philosophy, but when you ask them to pinpoint something significant and specific which they have changed their mind about as a result of their philosophical studies, they often find it hard to identify anything.

I can give you an example of a transformation in my life, and it's about death. At one stage I believed that at a certain point the soul leaves the body and goes to heaven. I certainly don't believe that any more. I don't have enough evidence to support that kind of exotic belief. The same is true of astrology. Philosophy gives you the tools to think critically about these things.

I think there's a reason why it might be difficult to put your finger on specific changes that are due to philosophy. It so infuses your way of thinking that you can't see what you were like before you studied it. Certainly, it has made me much more confident to challenge the arguments people are using. I'm not intimidated by politicians or experts in fields, because I can see the structure of the arguments they are using and see their techniques. Without having studied philosophy I might have been able to do that with some kind of incidentally acquired ability, but I've made a serious study of the structure of arguments and that has enabled me to think critically about what's going on when people advance arguments.

Another way in which it has transformed me is my unwillingness to tolerate bullshit. I no longer assume that because something's difficult to understand it must be profound; I don't give credit to people simply because they have got positions of eminence; I'm sceptical about experts being treated as authorities in other fields. All those sorts of things have really changed my life.

Has the writing you've done at the popular and introductory level had any effect on the research you do?

Looking back at things I wrote ten years ago, I think my writing style for research work has become more streamlined and I'm less likely to use technical terms for their own sake. My sentences are shorter. I also don't feel the need to make vast numbers of allusions to what has been written in the subject before. Certainly, writing *Thinking from A to Z*, which is about critical thinking, made me far more aware of argument structure and I hope that's paid off in my writing in other areas. I suppose my awareness of the difficulty of making any worthwhile contribution in philosophical research has contributed to the fact that I have devoted some of my time to writing about the history of photography, particularly about the photographer Bill Brandt. That's an example of a research area in which you don't have to be a genius to make an important contribution. I'm also working on a biography of an architect.

For me, the personal development from the writing I've done concerns what I thought I knew. Starting out to write *Philosophy: The Basics*, I thought that I knew quite a lot about all the different areas that were to be covered. But when I tried to explain them clearly to someone who didn't already know quite a lot about the area, I found that I really knew very little. In many ways, writing research articles is easier because you can take so much for granted – but, of course, that has its own dangers.

I've always thought that philosophy is in some sense about its fundamentals. In some subjects, such as mathematics, if you've got to an advanced level and then return to a beginners class, you don't learn anything. But if you are forced to think and write clearly about the most basic things in philosophy, it's somehow an important and worthwhile thing to do. Is that a view you have sympathy with?

I think academic specialisations within philosophy can have the effect that some people are extremely good within their narrow field, but have scant knowledge of what goes on in other areas of philosophy. In some cases, they have very little awareness of some of the basic arguments that have been advanced in the history of philosophy. It's quite common to find lecturers in philosophy who couldn't tell you what's in

Plato's most famous dialogues. That's quite shocking really. You might find that attitude to the history of the subject in the sciences – I recently read that the geneticist Steve Jones has yet to find a biology under-graduate who has read Darwin's *The Origin of Species*. But the great works of philosophy aren't just lying there as if in a museum to be admired through glass. They have the capacity to invigorate the pres-ent. So to ignore them like that is a very strange thing to do. It's intellectually sloppy not to learn enough about your subject to be able to teach it at an elementary level across a wide range of topics. And yet that's what happens.

So there's this very narrow specialisation and perhaps that's one of the causes of the inaccessibility of much academic philosophy. If you ask the researchers, they'll say, 'well it's such a difficult technical sub-ject. Inevitably it's not available to *hoi polloi*'. But look at the position of the physicist. Physics is a much more difficult subject on the whole, I have to say, and it's difficult for the layperson to grasp. And yet there have been some brilliant popularisers of physics. With a few notable exceptions, we haven't been so lucky in philosophy.

Are you going to do more of this kind of writing?

At the moment I'm working on four different books. There's a text-book on philosophy, aimed at first year undergraduates in universities. Surprisingly, for me, in Britain there's no competitor, no well-established text that's widely used for first year undergraduates. In America, there are many textbooks which are widely used, several of which are quite good. It's strange that British philosophers have been so reluctant to write and to use textbooks. I think it's a social phenom-enon. In Britain, for whatever reasons, people who acquire academic posts in philosophy become little kings or queens – usually kings – in their own kingdoms, and they determine how they teach their subject without interference from the other kings in their kingdoms next door. So the person assigned to teach aesthetics, for example, may have a particular take on the subject and may construct the curriculum in a completely idiosyncratic way. The student who is on the receiving end of that emerges having studied the subject only from that angle. That would be intolerable in many academic disciplines, but that's the way it has happened traditionally in philosophy. People who have set themselves up in this way are reluctant to change because it's easier to carry on in those grooves. So they're reluctant even to consider the idea that a textbook might be useful to them. Fortunately, however, with an influx of younger lecturers, these sorts of attitudes are gradually changing.

The other three books I'm working on at the moment are: *The Art Question*, which is about philosophical attempts to define art; a biography of the modernist architect, Ernö Goldfinger; and *Essay Writing: The Basics*.

Select Bibliography

Philosophy: The Classics, 2nd edition, Routledge, 2001
Reading Political Philosophy: Machiavelli to Mill (with Matravers and Pike), Routledge, 2001
Thinking from A to Z, 2nd edition, Routledge, 2000
Freedom: An Introduction with Readings, Routledge, 2000
Philosophy: The Basics, 3rd edition, Routledge, 1999

Appendix: Rationale and Purpose

Who's In and Who's Out

The vibrancy in British philosophy which we identified in the Introduction is mostly a product of a generation of philosophers currently in their thirties and forties. From this generation will emerge the philosophers who will occupy the most senior positions in the subject over the next decade or so. They are the heirs to philosophy's aristocracy. It is, therefore, on this generation, rather than their seniors, that we have focused. Their elders include many notable philosophers, a lot of whom have responded to the changes in the subject that have been driven by their successors. But, as it is the younger generation which most embodies the new spirit of philosophy and which will lead the subject in the years to come, it seemed most appropriate to focus on them to capture the mood of philosophy in Britain today.

This means that the philosophers in this volume have tended to be young – at least in philosophical terms. But it is not youth per se which was our guiding principle. No birth certificates were checked or age limits imposed. What we were looking for were people who represented this generation of thinkers, not philosophers who fell within a strict age limit.

A similar principle governed the British component of the

selection criteria. Again, no passports were presented by those invited for inclusion in the book. What we were looking for were philosophers who could be very clearly located within the cultural milieu of British philosophy today. This means that all the people included are working, and have predominantly worked within the community of British philosophy, and hence their work reflects the state of the subject we are trying to present in the interviews.

The quality of the work produced by the philosophers included in this book was a key consideration. The list of invitees (all of whom accepted) was drawn up by consultation with peers in the profession. But this does not mean that we have assembled 'the best sixteen young British philosophers'. While we do believe that this book contains interviews with the few undoubted stars of their generation, we would not for one moment suggest that our list comprises a definitive premier league of philosophers. Our aim was simply to gather together a representative range of the brightest philosophers from this group. We are sure, however, that this will not prevent some entertaining but spurious debates erupting as to who we should have left out and who we should have included.

Why Interviews?

Although there have been several published volumes of philosophical interviews, the format remains relatively unusual. In a sense, this is understandable. The rigour of philosophical argumentation requires the kind of control that is available in a monograph or journal article, but which is absent in other formats. Nevertheless, the interview format does offer a number of advantages that are pertinent in terms of what it is hoped that this book will achieve.

One advantage of the interview format is that it allows the philosopher to trade control for freedom. This extra freedom enables the philosopher to talk in a way which is different from their usual mode of address. This has a number of significant consequences.

First, professional philosophy, more often than not, deals in the minutiae of technical arguments. The interview format, in contrast, provides an opportunity for the philosopher to paint in broad brush strokes. For example, the philosophers interviewed for this book were able to reflect on the broad state of philosophy, on how their particular subdisciplines are viewed, and on the relationship between their work and society at large.

Second, a philosopher writing for a journal will be aware of the need to qualify every argument carefully and to ensure that their logic is absolutely tight. To be deficient in either of these areas is risky, both in terms of whether the article will be accepted for publication and in terms of its reception. But this does not apply with the interview format, since it does not form part of their 'research output'. Consequently, there is a freedom to try out arguments that might otherwise never have been voiced, and to express opinions without worrying about whether they meet professional standards of justification.

Finally, in an interview the philosopher is at liberty to drop the technical language of their particular field. Even if it is true that philosophers should as far as possible avoid getting bogged down in jargon in all their writing, it is undoubtedly a lot easier to do so in a situation where they're not expected to employ it. The significant point here is that as a result of talking more clearly, the ideas that the philosopher wishes to communicate become more readily accessible for a wider audience.

A further advantage of the interview format is that a monograph or journal article, unless it is specifically written for a general audience, will only ever be of interest to a narrow group of people – more than likely, the specialists of a particular subdiscipline within philosophy. The situation is entirely different with a book of interviews such as this one. Partly this has to do with the point made earlier about the non-technical nature of the conversations. However, it also has to do with the kinds of things that philosophers might be inclined to talk about when they're being interviewed. In monographs, and especially journal articles, it is unusual to find a philosopher engaging in any meta-analysis of the state of philosophy and their particular subdiscipline, as they have done in many of these interviews. Consequently, the book should be of interest to all professionals working in the field.

A final advantage of the interview format is that philosophical dialogue has a different character to monologue. If you're interviewing someone, then it is possible to ask them for clarifications, to press them on particular points, to ask them questions that might not have been expected, to get them to reflect on how their arguments fit together *in toto*, and so on. The result is a different mode of philosophising than that characteristic of a monologue (and, indeed, a philosophical dialogue, written by a single person). When it works well, the philosophical interview brings a freshness and spontaneity to philosophy that is frequently lacking, for example, in the rigours of a journal article. In this sense, the philosophical interview is valuable, in and of itself, as a mode of philosophising.

It is worth pointing out that some of the benefits of the philosophical interview accrue directly to the person being interviewed. For example, a number of the philosophers interviewed for this book said afterwards that the interview allowed them to get a better sense of how their work fitted together as a whole, and a better grasp of themselves as philosophers.

As was mentioned earlier in this book, John Searle has claimed that if you can't say something clearly, then you probably don't understand it yourself. In an interview situation, it very quickly becomes clear to the philosopher if the ideas that they're talking about are not being understood. If Searle is right, then the effort required to address this situation is worth it, not only because it means that the philosopher's ideas will have wider accessibility, but also because it is likely to increase their own understanding of what their philosophical claims entail.

Further Reading

Borradori, G., *The American Philosopher: Conversations with Quine, Davidson, Putnam, Nozick, Danto, Rorty, Cavell, MacIntyre and Kuhn*, University of Chicago Press, 1994

Magee, B., *The Great Philosophers*, 2nd edition, Oxford Paperbacks, 2000

Magee, B., *Men of Ideas*, BBC, 1978

Pyle, A. (editor), *Key Philosophers in Conversation*, Routledge, 1998

Tobias, M., J. Patrick Fitzgerald and D. Rothenberg (editors), *Parliament of Minds: A Philosophy for a New Millennium*, State University of New York Press, 2000

Yancy, G. (editor), *African-American Philosophers: 17 Conversations*, Routledge, 1998

Further material relating to the interviews in this book can be found on *The Philosophers' Magazine* web site, at:

www.philosophers.co.uk/britphil/

Index

Index